OUR RELIGIONS

by

CHENG TE-K'UN
DAVID GOLDSTEIN
H JOHN LEWIS
MARJEET KAUR
MOHAMMAD NASEEM
DHARAM K VOHRA
RUSSELL WEBB

Editor: Harold A Guy

J M Dent & Sons Limited
Bedford Street   London

Made in Great Britain
at the
Aldine Press · Letchworth · Herts
for
J M Dent & Sons Limited
Aldine House Bedford Street   London

ISBN 0 460 09558 7

Contents

PREFACE   vi

chapter 1   The Hindus   BY DHARAM KUMAR VOHRA   1
*Immigrants' Liaison Officer, City of
Bradford Police*

2   The Buddhists   BY RUSSELL WEBB   23
*Honorary Secretary of the London Buddhist
Vihara and joint editor of the 'Buddhist
Quarterly'*

3   The Chinese   BY CHENG TE-K'UN   40
*Reader in Chinese Archaeology, University of
Cambridge*

4   The Shintoists   BY H. JOHN LEWIS   62
*Formerly of the Society of the Sacred
Mission, Kobe, Japan, now Bishop of
North Queensland*

5   The Jews   BY RABBI DR DAVID GOLDSTEIN   69
*Associate Rabbi, Liberal Jewish Synagogue,
London*

6   The Christians   BY HAROLD A. GUY   89

7   The Muslims   BY DR MOHAMMAD NASEEM   104
General practitioner

8   The Sikhs   BY PAMELA WYLAM (MARJEET
KAUR)   120
Editor of the Sikh Courier

POSTSCRIPT   133

A TABLE OF DATES   135

INDEX   136

Preface

So many books have been produced in recent years on
'world religions' that some may wonder if there is a place
for yet another. Such books generally present one individual's account of several religious systems—inevitably
from an outsider's point of view, however impartial a
writer may seek to be. The chapters in this book, on
the contrary, have been written by those who have first-
hand knowledge and experience of the faiths which they
describe:

A Hindu lecturer who is concerned with the welfare of
immigrants in a northern city in Britain;
A London business man who for the past twelve years
has been a Buddhist;
A Chinese scholar who is an authority on the history
and traditions of China;
A former resident in Japan who has made a study of
Shinto;
The Rabbi of a synagogue in north London;
A Muslim doctor in Birmingham;
An English woman teacher who is a member of the
Sikh community.

Most of these contributors give their allegiance to the

systems which they describe; they write of 'our religion', speaking for the community to which they themselves belong. In another sense also this is a book about *our* religions. People in many countries are becoming conscious that, with the modern facilities for travel, a multi-racial society is developing in their midst which is bound to be also a multi-religious society. There is considerable misunderstanding about some of these religions and their adherents, much of it arising from sheer ignorance. The question is asked, sometimes in a spirit of genuine enquiry and sometimes in exasperation, 'Who are these people?' This book is an attempt to answer this question. It is not so much about religions and -isms as about people. It is hoped that the accounts which are given here may lead to a more sympathetic understanding of these minority groups and an appreciation of the value of the beliefs which they hold, the practices in which they take part and the principles which guide their lives.

I should like to express grateful thanks to all the contributors and an appreciation of the willing co-operation they have shown at each stage in the production of this book. Thanks are also due to the staff of the Education Department of Messrs. J. M. Dent & Sons Ltd, without whose interest and encouragement the completion of this book would not have been possible.

H. A. G.

Worcester

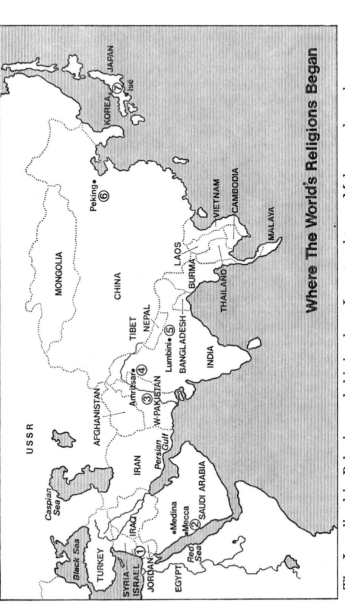

Where The World's Religions Began

1 The Jews lived in Palestine and this is where Jesus taught. 2 Mohammad was born near Mecca. 3 The first Hindus lived by the river Indus. 4 Guru Nanak founded the Sikh religion in the Punjab. 5 Gautama, the Buddha, was born in north India. 6 Confucius and Lao-Tzu taught in China. 7 The home of Shintoism is Japan.

1

The Hindus

The term Hindu is derived from the word 'Sindhu' (the river Indus) and it originally had a territorial significance implying residence in a particular area of India. About 2500–2000 B.C. the Aryans, a resilient wandering people who spread from the central steppes of eastern Europe, came to the Indian sub-continent through Persia and the high passes of Asia Minor. These earliest founders of Hinduism settled in the north-west frontier of India and the province of Punjab and from there the civilisation flowed into the valley of the Ganges and by slow degrees extended over the whole of India. The Aryans conquered, settled and finally integrated with the indigenous race of darker-skinned Dravidians, with their own culture and traditions, who moved eventually further south. Thus Hinduism came to include a vast variety of people.

During the course of history Hinduism has undergone various changes from age to age and in different communities, yet its spirit has remained the same. It has easily absorbed the customs and ideas of the people with whom it has come into contact and among whom it has spread. Although Hinduism has many sects and includes various creeds and notions, it has been a spiritual force which has embraced their different forms and mysteries and moulded them into one organic whole. In spite of differences among the sects, the Hindus remain a distinct cultural unity, with common history and mutual tolerance. Hinduism welds them all together to live in peace and harmony.

Hinduism has the support of records four to five thousand years old, which themselves might have taken more than four millennia to accumulate before they were recorded in writing. The sacred books of the Hindus are the Vedas, the Upanishads, the Puranas and the Epics.

The Vedas are records of the way of life of the Aryans, their mystical hymns of praise and their beliefs. They consist of ancient hymns and prayers to the gods and are four in number—the Rig Veda, the Yajur Veda, the Sam Veda and the Atherva Veda. These are the earliest literary monuments of Hinduism and constitute the basis of the Hindu religion. The Rig Veda is the oldest of the four, its earliest hymns having been recorded between 4000 and 2500 B.C. It is a compilation of 1017 hymns in praise of the deities. The compositions are in specific metres and are intended for loud recitation. The hymns of the Yajur Veda are in prose, for recitation in lower tones at the yajna—oblation, adoration and worship.

The Vedas (the word is taken from the Sanskrit root *vid*, meaning knowledge) are the utterances of inspired seers known as Rishis, claiming contact with transcendental truth. They are accepted as the most sacred spiritual store of knowledge as conceived by the Rishis. They are also known as Shruti (from a root meaning to hear or to listen), for the knowledge was revealed or communicated to the Sages orally. This also implies that the knowledge of the Vedas was passed to the student as he listened attentively to the Guru—the teacher. The Vedas are accepted as final authority by all the different Hindu sects and this common link helps to unite the various creeds. The Vedic traditions and thought live in the Hindu spirit as much now as ever before. Even Buddha, who revolted against the Hindu authority of his day, accepted the Vedic truths as eternal.

The utterances of the Vedas are the expression of spiritual experience and practice. Throughout the history of Hinduism a correlation of experience and experiment has been considered an essential element in further progress. By questioning different religious concepts and relating them to our lives, we can distinguish the sound from the unsound, the true from the false, the everlasting from the momentary. What every Hindu searches for in the Vedas is the higher truth and deeper significance that lies behind the 'word of the Veda' itself. We look for the spirit of the law of the universe.

Our knowledge extends as our experience and our theology develop. The Hindu philosophy of religion is based upon experiment as well as experience. There is no emphasis on 'Thou shalt' or 'Thou shalt not'. Hinduism, not betrayed into enunciating final commandments, has left the human spirit free to experiment in mental and spiritual matters whenever and wherever it wants. The Hindu thinker readily admits another's point of view and is always prepared to consider this as worthy of attention. This is the spirit of the Vedas.

The Upanishads are another store-house of the spiritual knowledge which is essential in order to open the eye of the soul which is veiled by Maya or illusion, leading to the knowledge of the Eternal and the complete realisation of the freedom of the human spirit from bondage. The word Upanishad means 'knowledge from a competent preceptor or teacher'. These books, written in Sanskrit, are in the form of dialogue between Guru and pupil and are full of deep spiritual knowledge.

The Upanishads deal with the subject with which the

3

spirit of man has been grappling from the very beginning of human existence—the nature of God. Is he with qualities or without? Is he knowledge or reason or bliss? Is he existent or non-existent, a reality or an illusion or an invention of the human mind? What is the soul and what is its relation with God and the body in which it dwells? What is death? Is there a rebirth and, if so, why? Is there an identity of man's spirit with God? Can they ever be one or is this only a dream of the human mind? Other matters dealt with are ethics, wisdom, karma, the act and its consequences, the evolution of life and its destiny.

Tradition acknowledges the existence of more than one hundred Upanishads (written about 800 B.C.) but most of them have disappeared. Only fifty of them were translated into Persian under the patronage of the son of the great Moghal king Shah Jahan. From Persian they were translated into Latin in A.D. 1801–2. The German scholar and philosopher Schopenhauer declared, when he read the translation, 'In the whole world there is no study so beneficial and elevating as that of the Upanishads. It has been the solace of my life and it shall be the solace of my death'.

The Brahma Sutra—an explanation of the teaching of the Upanishads in the form of sutras or brief statements—is acknowledged to have been written by a teacher named Badarayan. In it he deals with the subject of Brahma, the origin of the world, the sustenance and the dissolution of the universe. It is philosophy tersely expressed, beyond the grasp of most laymen. The Puranas are the ancient books which contain legends and the traditional history of India. There are scores of Puranas, but the main ones are eighteen in number, supposed to have been compiled by the sage Vayas.

The Epics: the Ramayana and the Mahabharata
Hinduism has been influenced by these two epics more

4

than by any other sacred literature. The Ramayana is a poem consisting of 24,000 verses in seven books. Its authorship has been attributed to the sage Valmiki, royal priest of Dashratha, king of Ayodhya, modern Oudh, in north India. It was written in Sanskrit and dates from the ninth century B.C. In the sixteenth century A.D. the saintly scholar Tulsi Das wrote *Ram Charit Manas*—'The Lake of the Conduct of Rama'—using the original material of the Ramayana but in a different arrangement and metrical variety.

The characters in the Ramayana are ideal as much as historical. Many characters represent a type which a Hindu should strive to attain. Rama, prince of Ayodhya, is an incarnation of Vishnu, one of the trinity of Hindu godheads—Brahma, Vishnu and Shiva. Though an incarnation of a god, he is the ideal child, the ideal student and warrior, brave and compassionate. He is an ideal son, brother, husband and king, who has come down to earth with a novel code of morality and ethics. The version by Tulsi Das has made more impact on Hindu life, not only because of the authority and command of the subject matter, but also because of the arrangement of the material and the grace of the language.

The Mahabharata—sixth century B.C.—is one of the longest epics in the world, consisting of 240,000 verses. The book is an account of the battle fought between two families of cousins, the Kaurvas and the Pandvas, in the field of Kurukshetra in the north of India. Interpolated in the Mahabharata is an episode of eighteen chapters called the Bhagavad Gita or 'Song of the Lord', as it has been popularly known in the west. The author of the Gita elaborates on the different paths in the approach to Divinity. The book is a dialogue between God and the soul. From the idea of death there springs forth the concept of the immortality of the soul. The body is to the spirit what the clothes are to the body. The spirit is

5

eternal. 'Weapons do not cleave it; fire does not burn it; water does not wet it; nor does the wind make it dry.' In the Gita the essential philosophy of Hinduism is taught by the god Krishna to Arjun, the princely archer of the Pandvas, and the battle represents the conflict that rages within the spirit of mankind. He speaks of man's duty in this world, of the idea of renunciation, of selfless action dutifully undertaken without thought for the egotistical fruits of that action, of the yoga of personal self-discipline for its own sake and for no other motive, of liberation beyond the confining framework of human flesh into the realms of the spirit and imagination where all beauty and one-ness lie. In his introduction to the Gita Aldous Huxley maintained: 'The Gita is one of the clearest and most comprehensive summaries of the Perennial Philosophy ever to have been made. Hence its enduring value, not only for Indians but for all mankind.' Dr. S. Radhakrishnan writes: 'In the Gita are united the currents of philosophical and religious thoughts diffused along many and devious courses. Many apparently conflicting beliefs are worked into a simple unity to meet the needs of all time, in the true Hindu spirit, in the sense of a World Religion or *Vishwa Dharma*.' [1]

The Gita has a message that spiritual beings need not be recluses. 'The union with the Divine may be achieved and maintained in the midst of worldly affairs and the obstacles to that union are not outside us but within us.' This is the central theme of the Gita. We can find our way to the transcendental personality by concentration through various media. One of these is yoga. This word stems from the root *Yuj*, meaning to put together, harness or collate. The practice of yoga does not mean merely indulging in bodily exercise or contortions—with which the term is

[1] There are several editions of the Bhagavad Gita in English, including one in Penguin Books.

generally associated in the western mind—but the yoking together of all the mental, spiritual and physical potential in man. It sees the bodily postures as only a means to a much more comprehensive end. Through an efficiently run bodily system and properly concentrated breathing the mind can be so directed that body is finally forgotten. Yoga has nothing in common with escapism achieved by means of drugs. It is the discipline of the self for the sake of attaining a loftier stage. It is the harmonising of body and spirit, action and wisdom, feeling and intuition for the sake of renunciation when it may be required. It is a science which puts man the momentary close to man the eternal, the indestructible sublime of the universe. Through control of the bodily system one is freed from all earth-binding desires to such an extent that attainment is reached 'with the impersonal infinite from which all things arise'.

HINDU BELIEFS

Karma

This word is derived from the root *Kre*, which means to act or to do. The theory of Karma has been much misunderstood in the west. It has been associated with fatalism or determinism or predestination. Karma is none of these things. It is the law of cause and effect. At all levels, Hinduism is concerned with a continual dialogue between good and evil, right and wrong. Karma tells us that as in the physical world so in the moral and mental world there is law, which man has to follow. Every act, whether it is in the form of thought, word or deed, affects the personality of a man. This is the universal and immutable law. Man is a thinking animal. He has this higher status because he can choose between right and wrong, good and bad, ugly and beautiful. He can sow now what he wants to

7

reap in the future. Our past is facing us today; the results of today will appear tomorrow. Our acts can transform not only our own nature and our future, but also the future of the universe. Karma intensifies our sense of the tremendous importance of every decision we make for right or wrong. Every act bears fruit sooner or later—good from good and bad from bad. The law of Karma tells us not to expect bananas from a poisonous plant.

Karma asks that we should refrain from desiring the fruit, we should act without seeking reward. Says the Lord Krishna in the Bhagavad Gita: 'You are bound by duty to act only; if at all there is a fruit, leave it to me'. In the words of Kabir, a saint and poet (1440–1518), 'The dice, not the fruit, is in your hands. Throw the dice. Act.' It is a sacrifice to be done. The fruit must be left to the divine will. The doctrine of Karma encourages man's aspirations for true immortality. Even Buddhism, which in my view is part of Hinduism in a revolutionary sense, did not reject the Vedic theory of Karma. In the words of Sir Edwin Arnold, 'New life reaps what the old life has sown; where its march breaks off the new march begins; holding the gain and answering for the loss, in each life good begets more good, evil fresh evil' (Edwin Arnold: *The Light of Asia*, 1879).

Transmigration

The doctrine of Karma gives rise to the belief in transmigration of the spirit from one body to another and a deep rooted faith in life after death. In the Hindu theory of rebirth, the soul is born high or low according to its own merits and demerits. This is quite in conformity with the law of cause and effect which is the basis of the physical universe. Man is the architect of his fate. The good and the evil that befall a man cannot be explained if we confine ourselves to the present span of life. The moral requital can be upheld only by admitting transmigration of the

8

soul. This conviction makes the believer realise his responsibility for his present suffering and also gives him an incentive for right conduct in order to build up a happy future. As he accepts with serenity his present ill-fortune, he can look forward to the future with joy and courage.

'What happens after death?' has been a question since the dawn of history. The theory of total annihilation is not satisfactory, for it gives only a partial picture of existence and provides no meaning to life. The sages of the Upanishadas were not impressed by the alternative theory of eternal retribution or rewards in a hell or in a heaven. Such a view conceives a result which is disproportionate to the cause. 'Life on earth is short, exposed to error, bristling with temptation. Many of our wrongs may be due to a faulty upbringing. To inflict upon the soul eternal punishment for the error of a few years is to throw to the winds all sense of proportion. It is also inconsistent with God's love for his created beings.' It is acknowledged in Hinduism that each person is responsible for his own deeds. We hold in our hands the chain to eternity. Life is always there. 'The sun which sets here rises elsewhere.' Death is no longer an object of fear. When a man, through repeated rebirths, has fulfilled all his desires, he achieves everlasting satisfaction. He lives in communion with Brahma—God.

The doctrine of transmigration according to karma has exercised a deep influence on millions of Hindus and also on people of other faiths. It has brought to the Hindu a firm optimism. Hindu literature from the Vedas onwards has been full of hope and joy, courage and optimism—until Hinduism came into touch with materialistic western thought. 'The sedge has' never 'withered from the lake.' The birds have always been singing. 'Every saint has a past' is accepted, yet with the belief also that 'every sinner has a future'. We do not believe that the world is a place where 'but to think is to be full of sorrow'. We are in full agreement with Shelley—'If winter comes, can spring be far behind?' Wordsworth's *Ode on Intimations of Immortality* is not only a source of poetic delight but a message of conquest over death.

THE CONCEPTION OF GOD

The Hindu philosophers were very familiar with the variety of the concepts of God. The Hindus believe that the Divine reveals itself to man within the framework of his own situation. Every man, therefore, is entitled to worship God by ways and means which appeal to his personality and in accordance with his racial or historical tradition. Each religious genius has spelled out the 'mystery of God' in accordance with his own approach. True religious experience can lead us to the understanding of the variety of the pictures of God. A refined definition of God as a moral personality and holy love may contradict cruder ideas which look upon him as a despot, but they all refer to the same reality. Hinduism is not opposed to the revelations and prophets of other religions or the varied forms in which God may appear.

The main personal gods in Hinduism are a trinity of Brahmā, Vishnu and Shiva. Brahmā is the creator, the manifestation of the abstract idea of divinity. Brahmā himself is not much worshipped, though known to every Hindu and mentioned in every religious ceremony. Vishnu is the preserver and sustainer of the universe. God in the form of Vishnu is said to be the source, the transcendent God of the created worlds. Shiva is the source of creation and also of the ultimate destruction of the universe for the sake of reconstruction of the good. God in the form of Shiva is very popularly worshipped. He has an infinite number of attributes and powers, is free from all defects and faults, is Lord of the whole material and spiritual universe. He is the cause of the creation, maintenance and dissolution of the world and by his grace of the liberation of souls through the cessation of their bondage to the process of rebirth.

Western visitors to Indian villages notice an astonishing number of pictures of gods and goddesses. Hindu religion is therefore charged with being polytheistic. But the multiplicity of gods and goddesses is not polytheism. To the Hindu a variety of views of God does not mean there are many supreme personalities. In different ages to different people the divine is manifested in different ways and forms. All minds cannot think exactly alike. Other people may have their own chosen deities but there need be no conflict. 'Only one God pervades all beings in the universe' goes the Hindu saying. The main spirit behind all images and pictures is called by different names, but they mean the same thing to every Hindu, whatever his caste, creed or notion. Images are not 'gods'. They are symbols and an aid to worship. They are the lights on a dark road in the middle of night when we grope for our destination; the stars to lost ships rolling over the vast waters of the universe. The Hindu regards the content behind the picture, image or idol, rather than the idol itself. 'The lights are needed as long as it is dark. When the sun rises the lights become of no use.'

Alain Danielou, the author of *Hindu Polytheism*, says: 'Hinduism or the "Eternal Religion", as it calls itself (*Sanatan Dharma*), recognises for each age and for each society a new form of revelation and for each man, according to his development, a different mode of worship, a different morality, different rituals and different gods. . . . Therefore there is little room in Hinduism for dogmas, for proselytism, for set rules of behaviour'. The message of Hinduism is one of tolerance and understanding. 'God is one; the sages name him variously' (Rig Veda 1.164.46).

Hinduism firmly accepts that some of the richest

religious manifestations require a personal God. While the personal aspect of the Supreme is valid, the super-personal Reality must not be forgotten. 'When we emphasise the Reality in itself, we get the absolute God, but when we relate it to ourselves, God becomes personal.' The reality is not the tangible world we see around us in material terms but the illusive inner core of our beings. God is within each one of us in the very fact that we exist. Divinity is ourselves. The Sanskrit saying is: *Tat twam asi*—'Thou art That'. In the Hindu view there can be no atheists. No matter how much we deny God, we *are* God by the very nature of our creation.

Hinduism insists that we should strive steadily upwards and increase our knowledge and feeling of God's presence everywhere and in all beings. 'The cultivated ones always tolerate the beliefs of the inadequate ones and their lack of understanding.' It is the duty of the 'advanced' ones that in the name of toleration they should protect the superstitions, rites and customs of those whose pace towards the light is slower than theirs. The holy waters of Eternity have poured into a few spirits who must be allowed to let the waters flow to fertilise the barren tracts. Realisation of God without action will become stagnation. God has filled the world with variety and many glorious hues.

Incarnation

Hinduism is opposed to the idea that there is only one manifestation of the divine. God manifests himself through many different personalities and numerous prophets, in all ages of history, in all nations and races. The idea of Vishnu as God developed into two important forms of incarnation (Rama and Krishna) and many other *avtaras*, as the Hindus call them. The theory of avtaras, or extremely holy spirits born in human form, assumes divine concern for human endeavour. The avtaras are born not only to put down evil, but to teach mankind and to

12

establish 'codes of duty as they are needed,' as Krishna says in the Gita; 'I appear in different forms in different ages'. To accept that the message of one seer, one prophet or of one religion is the last and the only one to be true is to circumscribe God's personality and light.

Worship (Puja)

Although every religion professes to accept God's omni-presence, yet he seems by some to be confined to particular places and buildings for worship. As far as the Hindus are concerned, there is no specific place of worship, nor is there any precise method of worship. Since God is every-where, worship can be conducted at any time, at any place, in any way. 'God lives neither in heaven nor in the heart of the yogin; wherever his devotees sing his prayer, he is there' (Narad Sutra 16–19). Worship is as myriad in its forms and variety as there are individual Hindus. In the preliminary stages of our pursuit of the divine our minds are generally distracted. The Hindu finds a medium through which he can focus his mind on the abstract and higher aspects of divinity. For the sake of concentration, images are an aid for those whose minds are not yet stable and firm. When the mind has achieved stability, no image is needed. Then we can tell the diamond from the stone; we shall not mistake the eternal for the transient. We hold Reality in our hands.

'They will never be able to describe the joy from the new experience and the grandeur of God when they stand face to face with him.' To describe this accurately is beyond the power of human speech. To try to explain this spiritual experience is, in the saint Kabir's words, 'like a dumb man with a lump of sugar in his mouth'. It does not matter whether the individual has seen the Light by knowledge or by devotion, in an image or without an image, whether through the teachings of the New Testa-ment, the Gita, the Quran or the Granth. The Hindu

13

believes in 'several ways leading to the same summit'. The names for God are different in language only. They are all one.

Marriage

Marriage has never been thought of as a matter of convenience in Hindu history. It has not depended on 'falling in love', as we know it in the west, neither has it always been a matter for parents to arrange. The Puranas, the Ramayana, the Mahabharata and other more recent books which have influenced the structure of Hindu society speak repeatedly of 'Savayamvara'—marriage by individual choice. The marriage was subject to conditions imposed on the would-be husband either by the girl herself or through her parents. Polygamy has always been discouraged. In specific circumstances and exceptional situations another marriage has been allowed but this is not a privilege granted to everybody.

The practice of *sutti*—that a widow should burn herself on the funeral pyre of her dead husband—has no place in the most ancient sacred literature and is not now practised in India. It is said to have originated about the year A.D. 1300, when king Khilji attacked the king of the Rajputs in north India in order to marry the queen, Padmani. When it appeared that the Rajputs were being defeated, the women built up a huge pyre and set it aflame and eight hundred of them, with Padmani at their head, burnt themselves alive in order to save themselves from falling into the hands of the conquerors. When the victorious Khilji entered the palace and searched for Padmani, he found only one old woman alive. When he asked in sign language where the queen was, the woman picked up a handful of ashes and scattered them towards the sky. This

14

practice of *sutti* became a terrible obligation for many a widow. It was forbidden by the British authorities during their administration of India.

Women have always been held in high esteem in Hindu society. One is amazed to see as many goddesses as gods in the Hindu pantheon. There are hundreds of goddesses. Hindu thinkers always gave women respect, although women in India never held a demonstration for equal rights. They have been and still are regarded primarily as concerned with the affairs of the home and as the bankers of the household. In Indian terminology a woman is called *ardhangni*, 'the half of the body' or, as the flattering English phrase has it, 'the better half'. All that belongs to the husband belongs to the wife also. Since delicate and heavy responsibility is given to a woman, it is essential that the man's companion must be of approximately the same mental and spiritual status.

The horoscope

The birth of a child is always a happy occasion. In most cases the family priest prepares the horoscope of the newborn baby. The horoscope shows the position of the planets which are said to influence the future of the individual. The subject is a controversial one, but the system means that a detailed recording must be made of the exact time and date of the birth, the parentage and the rest of the family tree.

In the villages, which represent the real India more than the cities, this system still prevails. Before a marriage the horoscopes of both parties are consulted and the hereditary factors are ascertained. The horoscope gives clear indication, especially in a closely knit society, of the kind of blood running in a particular group or family, of mental, physical and spiritual traits and an assessment of their future. The Hindus do not ignore heredity. Traits and faculties inherited from our parents certainly run through our blood and issue in the coming generation. The horoscope can tell what is suitable for each partner and consequently what the next generation can be expected to be like.

Cremation

The body is only an instrument by which the soul expresses its existence. The body is useful only as long as the soul lives in it. After the soul's departure the body is of no use. The Hindus therefore do not believe in burial; the body is cremated. There are some faiths in the world with a belief that the soul has to appear in the same body on the day of judgment to account for the wrongs of a lifetime. This idea does not appeal to the Hindu mind. Why cannot the same spirit take another body after one is torn and worn out? Why cannot it be given more lives and thus more chances to cast away the sins for which it is responsible?

After the body has been cremated, the remains are collected and taken by one of the relatives to be deposited in the river Ganges. One reason for the visits to these holy places is the belief that every Hindu family has a specific mould or lineage (*gotra*) and each *gotra* has a priest of its own at the river Ganges at Hardwar (the 'Gateway to God'). The visitor, on leaving the railway train, is met by the priests who ask: '*Kaun kul, kaun gaon?*' —'Which family and which place of residence?' The visitor is accordingly directed to the proper family priest, who records the visit of the person, the reason for the visit and the names and brief history of those who have not been previously recorded there. This material is then included in an ancient record book, sometimes eight to ten feet long, and the visitor can see at a glance the entire family tree spreading over ten generations.

Another reason for these visits is that they constitute a psychological healing of the wounds which the death of a dear relative has inflicted on the mind. A very large percentage of the visitors to Hardwar make the journey with hearts heavy with grief. They meet people who have come with the same experience of pain and suffering and speak together of death, the common destiny of man in the flesh. They realise that they are not the only sufferers, there comes peace and the thought expressed in the common saying: 'There he goes from where he came, from waters of eternity to the waters of eternity'.

Music

This holds a significant place in Hindu life and worship. On occasions such as the birth of a baby, an engagement, a marriage, the opening of a new trade centre and especially in worship in the temples and other places, classical Indian music has always been a necessity. From the beginning of the Vedic period until now it has developed in various forms, both vocal and instrumental. A 'raga' consists of a few fixed notes chosen from anywhere in an octave. The musician will start from any one of the chosen notes and, after playing a brief composition, will return to the note he had started from. He will illustrate different approaches and expressions. Within the framework of the raga he will move in the lower or upper octave, exploring and producing new variations, but all the while being controlled by the rhythm kept by the drummer. Indian classical music is becoming more and more popular in the west. It has a special quality, feel and sensitivity, and a grace and depth which lift the spirit from ordinary levels to new heights. Western musicians like Yehudi Menuhin have felt this influence of the music of India.

The caste system

Much has been heard in the west of the caste system, but those who criticise it seem generally to be ignorant of the basic philosophy from which it springs. The origin of the caste system is described by Manu, who compiled a code of Hindu laws about the second century B.C., and is symbolised in the picture of Brahma. Manu maintained that the brahmins (the priestly caste) sprang from the mouth of Brahma, the kshatriyas (warriors) from his arms, the vaishys (farmers and merchants) from his stomach and the sudras (servants) from his feet. Manu held that the image of Brahma was the structure of society. It is like a body which is a systematic structure made of various limbs, sense organs and potentials, seen and unseen. Each organ of the body has a specific function to perform, in order to develop itself and the body as a whole. The arm cannot smell, nor can the feet eat. The tongue cannot hear and the heart cannot perform the function of the lungs. Each part of the body contributes its best to the whole and receives the best from the central core. The brahmins, who were said to have come from the mouth, were given the highest place in society because they were the fount of knowledge and the selfless guardians of the state. They were the guides. The arms or the shoulders are the symbol of power, which was held in the hands of the kshatriyas, whose function was to protect the interests of the state as a whole. The function of the vaishys was agriculture and trade and the sudras were the reserves for emergencies which might suddenly arise or other such functions. It was not very different from Plato's view of society, where he maintains: 'Only philosophers should be kings'.

The system may be compared with the situation in the western world, where a cobbler may advertise with pride that the same craft has been in his family for 150 years and people feel that work in his hands is more skilled than that of a new entrant into the trade. During the last few hundred years, however, the caste system has been seen to be damaging to the Hindu social structure. India has always been willing to accept fresh interpretations of old traditions. In our own time the spirit of Gandhi, Tagore and Vinobha Bhave has begun to stir people and the government of India has been busy in seeking to cleanse the Indian soil by destroying the dry roots of the caste system; but changes cannot happen overnight.

Ahinsa (non-violence)

To all creatures life is a dear possession; none of us wants to be deprived of it. Even an insect will sting for the sake of its life when it feels that someone is going to injure it. This gave Hindu thinkers the idea, or concept, of Ahinsa—non-killing, respect for life. This has been considered to be the greatest of all *dharmas* [1]. Violence breeds violence as greed breeds greed. Life is a gift granted to all of us by God and apart from him no one else has an authority to take it. Hindus believe that not only men and animals, insects and reptiles have life, but plants also. To destroy a plant is to kill it. The experiments of Sir J. C. Bose have suggested that plants can 'feel' and have reactions similar to those of human beings.

Non-violence stands first among the ten dicta inscribed on pillars which king Ashoka set up throughout his empire in the third century B.C. He was faced with a rebellion by the King of Kalinga and himself went to subdue the rebel king where he subsequently won the battle. During the evening following his victory he went to the battlefield, to measure the cost of his conquest. The sight of the dead and the cries of the helpless wounded made such an indelible impression on his mind that he solemnly pledged

---

[1] *Dharma* as commonly understood means religion. It is derived from the Sanskrit root *dhr*, which means to hold, to sustain or to grasp. In various ways it can mean quality, religion, justice, entity, merit, nature, right conduct, law and reality. In the Hindu view, whatever sustains the world is Dharma. All of us have an inner call towards a duty, which we must answer. We must act for justice, goodness and meritorious life and all that we do must be according to Dharma.

not to engage in battle any more and to establish a king-dom where all could live in peace and harmony. He be-came a follower of the Buddha and gave full imperial support to Buddhists to deliver their message to other countries.

Great men have suffered with patience and courage in their stand against the evils of society without giving vio-lence for violence, and the evil they fought against has often been exercised on them. Non-violence as preached by Gandhi did not appeal to some fanatics and the preacher of non-violence was himself shot to death. Socrates and Jesus faced the same fanaticism. Non-violence is not cowardice. It is sanctity practised with courage. It is respect for life; it is always more difficult to protect than to destroy. To preserve life is an heroic deed. Ahinsa is the greatest of virtues.

CONCLUSION

It is sometimes said that India is a land of religions. It has indeed many branches of a single religion, Hinduism. Hinduism can claim no founder, no central authority, no institutional organisation, no creed. It comprises a living philosophy of the most profound kind, a temple ritual (which has often confused the foreigner), ancient traditions of social customs with four thousand years of development behind them and, more recently, sweeping movements of social reform.

Hinduism is a way of life, a philosophy and an art. It is a philosophy in the sense that 'philosophy is the flight of the spirit in the cosmos'. Hindu thought is universal rather than personal or individual. The Hindu religio-ethical code is a synthesis of spiritual experience and psycho-sociological experiment. Experience and experiment go hand in hand in every sphere of life, both in science and in art such as painting, music, sculpture and poetry.

The value of a work of art will be judged in so far as it represents the universal. The sage in the spiritual sphere expresses his inspiration in words as the painter does in colours on canvas. The true artist is freed from personal attitudes; 'to artistic perception it is all one whether we see the sunset from a prison or a palace'. This is precisely the Hindu approach to divinity. Art alleviates the ills of life by showing us the eternal and the universal behind the transitory and the individual. Spinoza was right to emphasize that 'in so far as the mind sees things in their eternal aspect, it participates in eternity'. This is the philosophy behind the image worship among the Hindus. The power of art to lift us above the day-to-day strife is found particularly in music and it is no wonder that this is held so highly in Hindu worship and life.

Hinduism insists that we must progress in our knowledge of God and the realisation of his presence everywhere. We walk on the road bearing our destination in mind, but we do not ignore the other travellers on the same road. Hinduism honours the point of view and experience of others like that of its own. It is foolish to discard the variety of hues which may be used by others. True religion is to see the eternal behind the transitory, the divine behind the human. This is the religion of those who love humanity, truth and wisdom—*Sanatan Dharma*, the eternal and universal religion.

FOR FURTHER READING:

G. T. Garrat: *The Legacy of India* (O.U.P.).
J. Mascaro: *The Bhagavad Gita* (Penguin Books).
S. Nikhilananda: *The Upanishads* (four books—Dent).
S. Radhakrishnan: *The Hindu View of Life* (Allen and Unwin).
K. M. Sen: *Hinduism* (Pelican Books).

D. K. Vohra: *East comes West* (Community Relations Commission).

R. C. Zaehner: *Hindu Scriptures* (Everyman's Library— Dent).

FOR INFORMATION:

Mrs. Peggy Holroyde, Yorkshire Committee for Community Relations, Charlton House, Hunslet Road, Leeds.

Dr. T. O. Ling, 27 Cookridge Lane, Leeds.

2

The Buddhists

The teachings of Buddhism originated with one man, who lived in northern India five hundred years before the birth of Christ. The same century that threw up such towering thinkers as Pythagoras in Greece, Confucius and Lao-Tse in China, Zoroaster in Persia and the Second 'Isaiah' among the Jews also produced a figure in the sub-continent of India who was destined to transform radically the social and religious life of the people to a greater extent than any before or since.

The man so destined was born about 560 B.C. as Siddhattha Gotama (or Gautama), the only son of Suddhodana, a minor monarch of one of the many kingdoms and republics that were to be found throughout the country, which was not united under one central administration. The place of his birth was Lumbini, just inside the borders of present-day Nepal. As befitted a crown prince, Siddhattha was brought up in all the luxuries that society could then produce, but there was another and more significant reason for this course as directed by the king, his father. In keeping with tradition, the court astrologers and chaplains were summoned at his birth to predict the future of the infant prince. They all stated that should he remain in the world he could become an influential and powerful monarch, but should he renounce the world then he would attain to enlightenment (Buddhahood) and assist a suffering and ignorant mankind. It is recorded, however, that the youngest of the sages who were present firmly pronounced that the prince's destiny was to renounce the world.

Suddhodana understandably did all in his power to ensure that his heir would never for a moment be tempted to leave his comfortable, if artificial, surroundings. Gotama grew up always in the society of young, healthy and highly cultured companions; music, dancing and other pleasures and recreations were always available. The king gave strict instructions that no elderly, ill or disabled people were to be allowed in his son's presence.

As was to be expected, this state of affairs could not continue for ever and tradition tells of the dramatic means by which Siddhattha was made aware of life as it really was. On four occasions his charioteer drove him on pleasure trips outside the palace grounds. On these drives Siddhattha witnessed four sights that changed his whole outlook on life—an old man bent double with arthritis, a young man disfigured by a skin disease, a corpse being carried to the charnel ground and an ascetic monk collecting alms from lay disciples.

On returning to the palace Siddhattha reflected deeply on what he had seen. He felt a deep sense of frustration at being confined in a 'gilded cage', at the futility of his pursuit of pleasure when outside so many people existed without hope of succour of either a spiritual or a material kind. He thereupon resolved to quit his home. His one regret was the thought of leaving his wife Yasodhara—a cousin married to him at sixteen—and his baby son Rahula. However, his mind was made up and, at the age of twenty-nine, he secretly left the palace, garbed himself in the robes of an ascetic monk and entered a nearby forest to pursue his search for the meaning of life.

The society into which Siddhattha was born was broadly divided into four main sections or castes. These were sanctioned in the Vedic texts of the Hindu religion, the earliest sacred writings of India. The self-appointed spiritual guardians were the *Brahmins*, who officiated at the animal sacrifices which were performed to propitiate the many deities which were assumed to exist and maintain the universe in being. Next came the *kshatriyas* or warrior class, then the *vaisyas* or merchants and last the *sudras* or serfs. Outside this hereditary system, which is still to be found rigidly existing in many parts of India today, came the most despised section of the community, the *chandalas* or outcastes, who eked out a precarious existence by scavenging and performing other similar menial tasks.

Spiritual life in Hinduism had long been stagnant. Religious teaching was confined to the rituals, hymns and prayers contained in the four *Vedas* and known only to the Brahmins. There was, however, a widespread awakening in the sixth century B.C., when the two middle classes, the warriors and the merchants, asserted their independence of the pretentious claims of the hereditary priests. The keynote of this reformation was an emphasis on a life of renunciation. A householder could in fact lead a partially renounced, ascetic life hitherto but only after he had reared a family and put his business affairs in order. Now, however, if a man was a serious seeker after truth, he was expected to leave the worldly life altogether. Joining together in the forests, many such persons lived on the generosity of lay disciples—although their only want was food, and little enough of that—and they practised the most severe austerities. It was felt that only through self-mortification could the real Self be purged of physical restraints and be united in spirit with the *Brahman*, the divine essence that underlay the universe. The teachings of these ascetics have come down in the form of the Hindu books called *Upanishads*. It is questionable how much of the influence of this movement was felt by the people at large. The rising mercantile class, hard-headed and practical, required something much more radical and down-to-earth and, as will be seen, it was this group which gave the most fervent support to the teaching developed by Gotama.

Siddhattha, now an ascetic, keeping to the time-honoured custom, sought out the most renowned teachers of wisdom and meditation. Under them he mastered all the knowledge they could impart and gained proficiency in their yogic methods of mental training, leading to spiritual calm and inner peace. But in spite of this progress Gotama was convinced that there was far more to learn and understand about man, life and the universe. Hence he moved away from the gathering of disciples and adopted a solitary life in the forest. For six years he practised the most extreme forms of bodily self-torture, until he was reduced almost to a skeleton. Then there arose one of the many insights which were to distinguish him from all his contemporaries; he realised that, far from producing wisdom, mental clarity or release from physical or mental temptations, self-mortification only weakened the body and dulled the mind. As a prince, he had already indulged in and then repudiated the other extreme, hedonism, a life of pleasure, and Gotama now became convinced that there must be a middle way between these extremes.

He resumed eating sensibly, to the disgust of five disciples who had gathered under him; they assumed that their teacher had given up the struggle and admitted defeat. Undeterred, Gotama quietly pursued his search for truth and peace. Finally, at the age of thirty-five, while he was sitting cross-legged under a banyan tree at Gaya—the holiest place to Buddhists throughout the world—on the full moon day of May (*Vesākha*), his mind was completely illumined and transformed. He was enlightened, 'fully awakened'; he became the Buddha (a title derived from *bodhi*, wisdom). His mind was completely liberated from mundane attachments and sensual temptations. He had attained the supreme goal, *Nibbāna* or *Nirvāna*.

After much self-examination, the Buddha decided to reveal his new-found knowledge to the world and journeyed to Benares where an open-air venue for rival spiritual teachers was to be found in the nearby deer park at Sarnath. On arrival he was joined by his five earlier disciples, whose initial reluctance to meet him was overcome by the sight of his radiant expression and by his obvious understanding and concern for their welfare.

The teaching of the Buddha

Following this reunion the Buddha proclaimed his *Dhamma* —teaching, law, doctrine—on the full moon day of July (*Asālha*). The subject of his first sermon is literally translated as 'The setting in motion of the wheel of the law' and thenceforth the wheel became the symbol of Buddhism.

What was it that Gotama discovered? What had he realised? Why was he no longer under the sway of worldly desires and aspirations, summarized in the term *Māra*?

There are two extremes to be avoided, said the Buddha —self-indulgence and self-mortification, both of which are seen as vulgar, painful and unprofitable. The way to follow is that of the middle path, which produces light, knowledge, dispassion, release—*Nibbāna*. The Buddha then enunciated the Four Noble Truths or propositions. These are the very crux and essence of Buddhist teaching, from which everything else is really commentary, adapted for people of different dispositions, ages and places.

THE FOUR NOBLE TRUTHS

The first Truth is that all compounded things are, by their very nature, in a state of *dukkha*. There is no exact English equivalent for this term. It may be rendered as dissatisfaction, frustration, anxiety, suffering, pain. The following events and relationships are described as being characterised by *dukkha*: birth, old age, illness, death, association with people whom one dislikes, separation from those whom one loves, inability to get what one wants. It is important to note that the Buddha never denied that such experiences as happiness and enjoyment occur in our lives but held that by their very definition these terms must presuppose their opposites. All life is characterised by three states: *anicca* (impermanence, flux, change), *dukkha* and *anatta* (the insubstantial nature of compounded things, non-self or ego). The realisation of the truth underlying these propositions is the foundation of Buddhist teaching.

The second Truth is that this unsatisfactory state of things has been brought about by *tanhā*—desiring or craving for material possessions or for mental delights— by our clinging on to things without realising their transient nature or that each want or desire, far from being satisfied, will inevitably lead on to wanting even more distractions. Most people delude themselves into thinking that possessions are the essence of civilised life and advancement, whereas in reality they are simply the outward signs of affluence or accumulated wealth. Buddhists are expected, on the contrary, to remain content with whatever they have without forever hankering after new and superfluous possessions. The same can be said of mental distractions; rather than be continually on the lookout for new and original, time-consuming recreations, one should cultivate the mind of itself, calming it and being at peace with oneself.

The third Truth follows naturally on this. It states that this chain of grasping or attachment must be severed in order better to realise inner tranquility. This would effect a final cessation of *dukkha*.

The fourth Truth concerns the way or path leading to this cessation. This is divided into eight sections—the Noble Eightfold Path. These do not represent successive stages to be followed but are to be practised, understood or realised simultaneously. Since these comprise the essential Buddhist daily code of conduct it would be well to examine each section in some detail.

THE NOBLE EIGHTFOLD PATH

The eight steps of the Path fall into three sections—*sīla* (relating to morality, virtue, ethical training, restraint of the senses), *samādhi* (relating to concentration, meditation, mental training) and *paññā* (wisdom).

(*i*) *Sīla* comprises the three steps of right speech, right action and right livelihood. The first two may best be illustrated by reference to the Five Precepts (literally 'rules of training') which every lay Buddhist is expected to observe. He is to abstain from taking life or harming sentient beings; from stealing or misappropriating anything belonging to somebody else without asking permission; from misuse of the senses (e.g. addiction to time-killing pleasures); from 'false speech' (lying, swearing, slandering, gossiping); and from 'intoxicating drinks and sloth-producing drugs', which are prohibited because of their deleterious effects on the brain and other organs.

These may seem to be negative rules but there are also numerous positive exhortations of the Buddha. Thus, the Buddhist is expected to preserve life in all its forms; this does not necessarily mean that he has to be a vegetarian—this, like everything else in Buddhism, is a matter of choice. There is never any rigid rule or commandment in Buddhism, but simply a recommendation to practise certain skilful or wholesome courses of action which would lead to one's well-being. As a practical example, the Buddhist would oppose abortion but would condone birth control;

the first case results in the deprivation of life whereas the second implies prevention of a life to be born. Likewise in speech the Buddhist would always give truthful affirmations as discreetly as possible, use language pleasing to others, not be too talkative, keep silent at the right moment and seek to bring about concord where there is dissension.

'Right livelihood' originally referred to the 'five prohibited trades'—butchers, publicans, armourers, toxic producers and slave owners. All these involved taking or harming life in one way or another. One difficulty is that today, in our industrialised society, conditions of employment are so complex that an employee may discover that some product on which he is engaged at one end of a factory is being put to a wrong use, from the ethical standpoint, at the other end. One may safely say, however, that the good Buddhist would not hunt, shoot, fish, patronise blood sports, sell meat, drinks or poisons, engage in the manufacture of armaments or work in an advertising agency.

Apart from this negative aspect, there are also positive activities—'skilful' or 'wholesome' actions—which are encouraged in Buddhism. One of the most widespread and characteristic virtues of the Buddhist is generosity, *dāna*. This open-handed attitude stems naturally from the exhortation to be non-attached to material things. This does not mean that one is obliged to give away everything and live in penury. But wherever distress or need arises, Buddhists will flock round to relieve the suffering or collectively fulfil the want. Social welfare among Buddhists has always existed on a modest scale, inspired by the model Buddhist emperor Asoka, who united India in the third century B.C.

(*ii*) *Samādhi* comprises the two steps of right mindedness and right concentration. In Buddhism there is a carefully arranged scheme of mental training; the exact technical term is *bhāvanā*—'mental culture'—which connotes any factor which uplifts or purifies the mind. The Buddha was once asked to sum up his teaching in one word. He replied using the term *sati* (mindfulness). The Buddhist is asked to be aware of everything that he does, says or thinks, wherever he may be throughout the day. It is a mistake to suppose that a Buddhist is meditating only if and when he is sitting cross-legged. In Buddhist meditation centres one may strengthen this practice by means of deliberately slowing down one's usual physical responses, for example by walking or eating very slowly. This attitude assumes even greater importance in modern industrialised society where in the midst of an endless whirl of activity it becomes essential to maintain a state of balance.

'Concentration' implies the state of 'one-pointedness' of mind, when the mind is perfectly still and focussed on the mental object of one's choice. There are two main aspects of meditation: *samatha* or exercises producing a state of calm, and *vipassanā* or exercises producing insight into the nature of man and the world. An example of the former is being mindful of the inhalation and exhalation of the breath, without attempting to restrict in any way the free passage of air in and out of the body. If one becomes perfectly aware of just this process then eventually all extraneous thoughts will fade away, leaving the mind clear and undisturbed. An example of the latter is watching and analysing the thoughts coming into one's mind and being aware of their nature, whether they are 'good', 'bad' or 'neutral', whether the feelings which they arouse display any one of the three characteristics that often dominate our minds—greed, hate, delusion (or ignorance) —in varying degrees of intensity.

Besides these there are numerous practices in meditation to suit all natures. Those inclined to a spiteful disposition could meditate on loving-kindness, imbuing oneself with this feeling and then suffusing it to those around. Those of a greedy (or sensual) disposition would meditate on death or the impermanence of compounded things like the body. Those of a devotional frame of mind would recollect the qualities of the Buddha, his teaching and his Community of Disciples as examples of holy life. This includes not only the order of monks, but also the supramundane community of disciples, monk and lay, who have attained the supreme bliss of *Nibbāna*.

(*iii*) *Paññā* (wisdom) comprises the three steps of right understanding, right thought and right effort. To the Buddhist understanding means 'seeing things as they truly are', recognising for example that in spite of superficial appearances some things are essentially not of a permanent nature. One of the most important, indeed crucial, aspects of this step is the thorough comprehension of the body. All other religions assume a personal core or entity, a soul or *attā*, but the Buddhist analyses his body and sees it as a collection of mental and physical components, all of which arise and come together at a favourable moment (that is, at conception and birth) and dissolve at an unfavourable moment (that is, at death)—all unstable and impermanent, possessing no subtle essence which in some mysterious manner continues in a life after death (although this is not completely denied, as will be seen below).

The Hindu conception of *karma* (or *kamma*) must be considered here. Before the Buddha defined it on a personal level, it was interpreted in the sense of man's duty according to his caste, which was unalterable and was accepted as his destiny. Thus in the *Bhagavad Gīta* Arjuna is exhorted by the god Krishna to kill on the battlefield by virtue of his being a member of the *kshatriya* (warrior) caste. Gotama clarified the meaning of *karma* as denoting volitional or intentional action which was willed by body, speech or mind and which was inevitably followed by a corresponding effect (*vipāka*), either immediately in this life or in the next. Of course everything depends on the nature and gravity of the action performed; even if a man has murder in his heart, the result would be of negligible effect unless such a crime was actually carried out. Thus it might well be that a particular act has no corresponding effect at all. The form of life or sphere of consciousness that one arrives at depends largely on the previous *karma*. This may not follow at once. Criminals, for example, may not immediately feel the long-term effects of their evil lives by being born into states of deprivation (in 'hells' or by being born disabled in human form) nor may the virtuous be at once born into 'heavenly' realms or to influential positions in the human world.

The accumulation of *karma* results in a continuation of life in one form or another. This is because men normally have desires and aspirations—they are still clinging on to something—and this 'life force' is sufficiently potent to act like a dynamo generating the new current that flows on, carrying a man's impressions, hopes, likes and dislikes. All states, however, are held by the Buddhist to be impermanent and all beings must 'rise' and 'fall' on the ladder of existence until they realise the futility of it all and aspire to the supramundane state, which may be realised even here on earth—*Nibbāna*—where greed, hate and delusion are extinguished. Then, after the dissolution of the mental and physical aggregates, there is no more rebirth.

To resume consideration of *paññā*; right thought denotes all mental states of a pleasing and beneficial nature—towards oneself first and towards others. Some may see traces of selfishness in this order of priority, but how can one extend thoughts of love and compassion to others if he himself is bereft of such qualities?

Right effort, finally, is that quality which ensures the success of the foregoing practices, the essential ingredient of perseverance against all failures and temptations—the effort to maintain good qualities in the mind and to

encourage their continued presence, to expel the un-
desirable traits and prevent their return.

For the next forty years, until his decease at the age of
eighty, the Buddha walked through northern and central
India, teaching all classes of men who were attracted by
his practical 'do-it-yourself' philosophy of life. Countless
numbers became ardent followers, many becoming
ordained in his Community of Monks (*Sangha*)—the
oldest order of celibate monks still existing in the world.

The Buddha spoke in Pali, the common tongue, as
opposed to Sanskrit, the written language of the brahmins.
His words were transmitted orally until the first century
B.C., when they were finally written down in Ceylon. The
teachings had been codified immediately on his decease in
northern India and have become known as the Pali Canon
or *Tipitaka* ('Three Baskets'). This contains the *Vinaya*
(the regulations governing the *Sangha*), the *Suttas* (the
discourses of the Buddha to both monks and laymen) and
the *Abhidhamma* (the higher philosophical teachings that
were elaborated after Gotama's time).

Most readers will probably regard Buddhism as just
another 'religion'. This word has theistic connotations,
however, and is normally associated with certain theological and cosmological theories. Buddhism is unique in
that all the formal trappings of 'religion'—belief in a
supreme Being or creator God, efficacious rituals, sacred
mysteries and ceremonies, mediating priests—were totally
absent at its inception. In mediaeval India, however,
Buddhism came increasingly under the influence of
Hinduism and features such as the cult of images became
prevalent. It is true that the Tibetan school in particular
has adopted some of the features and practices of 'religion',
and local deities have assumed some importance in other

34

Buddhist countries, but these developments are admitted by Buddhist leaders to be of purely secondary value.

What had caused this seemingly radical departure from the system of ethics and philosophy of life taught by Gotama? The sixth century B.C., when the Buddha lived, was in India an era of scepticism, an age of 'reason'. The old gods lost their credibility with large numbers of people, particularly with the emerging and influential mercantile class. When men realised that the brahmins were not the only custodians of religious truths, there developed freedom of expression along different lines, some stressing theistic views and others favouring materialistic ideas. Gotama's doctrine or 'way' (*Dhamma*) was intended as a middle path between these extremes. Doubtless there were 'deities', but the positions they occupied in the higher, immaterial planes of consciousness were temporary and powerless, the results of charitable or meritorious actions (*karma*) in past lives on the human plane. A First Cause was dismissed by Gotama as being illogical and a supreme personal Being was seen as a delusion arising from an incorrect view of the world. Given sufficient willpower, concentration and encouragement, man could well attain mastery over his senses (including mind) and achieve perfection completely unaided by external agencies.

This, then, was the dynamic and radical message of the Buddha, but it was realised that such a way of life must appeal to the heart as well as the intellect, to the emotions as well as the mind. From earliest times therefore it was recommended that those of a devotional frame of mind would do well to make obeisance to three things: the image or representation of the Buddha, his bodily relics (many of which are enshrined in *stupas*, huge tumuli topped by a spire, the origin of the pagoda) and the bodhi tree, under which the Buddha attained enlightenment, branches of which have been transplanted throughout

35

the Buddhist world. The devotee would also be encouraged to go on pilgrimage to the four main sites associated with Gotama's final lifetime: the place of his birth in Nepal, the site of his enlightenment in Bihar, the deer park at Sarnath, near Benares, where his first sermon was preached, and Uttar Pradesh, where the Buddha passed away.

All lay Buddhists, however, are expected to pay their deepest respect to the Triple Gem—Buddha, Dhamma and Sangha—and appropriate stanzas have been composed for the purpose of emphasising their respective functions as supreme teacher, the teaching and its exemplars, these including not merely the ordinary monks of today, but comprising all those fully enlightened ones both in the past and the present. In the natural course of events temples and monasteries were erected and endowed, but it must be stressed that these are essentially by-products of a system of thought and ethics which has its primary appeal to the individual. The effects of the Buddha's teaching soon covered a wide field, as a result of the repudiation of the claims of the brahmins to exclusive rights to teach and the rejection of the caste system by Buddhists. Schools, colleges and hospitals were opened and maintained largely by the monks. Art by way of sculpture and painting took on new forms, although the image of the Buddha did not appear for some centuries.

The Buddhist king Asoka, who united India for the first time in the third century B.C., did much to consolidate the religion and encouraged its spread to neighbouring countries. His own son, Mahinda, went as a monk on a mission to Ceylon, which has been predominantly Buddhist ever since. As a result of a brahmanical reaction aided by unsympathetic rulers, Buddhism declined in India in later centuries and the Muslim invasions of the twelfth century A.D. delivered the *coup de grâce*. It was not until the late nineteenth century that favourable conditions led to a revival of Buddhism in India, but even so it is still a minority religion in the land of its birth.

Elsewhere, however, Buddhism flourished, in south-east Asia (Burma, Thailand, Cambodia, Laos and Viet-Nam) and also in northern and eastern Asia (Tibet, Mongolia, China, Korea and Japan). The temple became, as it still is in rural parts of south-east Asia, the focal point of the community, acting as school, welfare centre and rest home, in addition to its function as a place for religious services. Although the Buddhist would have his own shrine at home with an image of the Buddha flanked by candles, with flowers offered and joss sticks burnt before it, organised meetings have developed to cater for the needs of the people. When a Buddhist goes to the temple, usually on one of the lunar quarter-days, he will pay his respects before the central image and offer flowers and incense to it. He does this not because he expects to have a prayer or petition answered, but out of respect for the supreme teacher who has so clearly shown him the way to perfect peace and understanding. While there he will probably listen to a sermon by a monk and the chanting, in Pali, of benedictory verses by the monks.

On special occasions—the opening of a new temple, the unveiling of an image, a funeral or moving into a new house—the monks of the locality will be invited to the house and offered lunch. Following this, special verses will be chanted and sometimes all-night ceremonies of this nature are held with the monks taking their turns every two hours or so. Monks will officiate at a funeral, but not at a wedding—a civil and social contract which is regarded as a family affair. Whilst monogamy has long been prac-tised in Buddhist Asia, the attitude towards sexual matters has generally been more liberal than in the west. If a married couple find that they are incompatible, it is widely recognised that divorce is the best solution, al-though the whole family feels responsible should things go wrong in this way. The family is still a strong social unit in Asia and the individual Buddhist is expected to look after the interests of his relatives and dependants when they are old or infirm rather than expect the State to step in. The spirit of self-help and independence is everywhere stressed and this extends even to business dealings and relationships between men in all stations of society.

BUDDHISM IN THE WEST

Apart from West Germany, Buddhism has taken root more in Britain than anywhere else in the west. The Pali Text Society, London, was founded in 1881 with the specific aim of translating the Pali texts and making them available to the English speaking public. From the turn of the century groups began to be formed in order to put the teachings into practice. Today there are to be found Buddhist groups of varying size in nearly all the major towns and cities. In London there are two *vihāras* (temples -cum-monasteries), in Chiswick and East Sheen, as well as The Buddhist Society near Victoria station.

All such centres and societies hold regular public meetings. Most of the ten thousand adherents in this country are British-born, the few immigrant Buddhists being mainly from Ceylon and India.

FOR FURTHER READING:

PRIMERS

H. Saddhatissa: *The Buddha's Way* (Allen and Unwin).
Walpola Rahula: *What the Buddha Taught* (Gordon Frazer, Bedford)
W. F. Jayasuriya: *The Psychology and Philosophy of Buddism* (Gunesena, Colombo).
E. J. Thomas: *History of Buddhist Thought* (Routledge & Kegan Paul).

TEXTS

Narada: *The Dhammapada* (Maha Bodi Society of India, Calcutta).

Nyanatiloka: *The Word of the Buddha* (Buddhist Publication Society, Candy).

FOR INFORMATION AND LITERATURE

London Buddhist Vihara, 5 Heathfield Gardens, London W4 4JU.

3

The Chinese

To understand religion in China we must bear in mind that China was the world of Confucius (571–479 B.C.). The Chinese view of life was moulded to a very large extent by his teaching, which for some 2500 years the Chinese have tried to put into practice. Confucianism has its roots in the ancient Chinese tradition and is a reassertion of the Chinese philosophy of life. This Chinese outlook is an affirmation of life in the world of men, with human relations as its centre of interest. It is an assertion of the importance of human existence and effort and it considers living a harmonious life with one's neighbours as man's first duty. The Confucian way of thinking is related, therefore, to actual existence or the concrete facts of life. It does not go in for abstract speculation or discussion.

It is hardly justifiable to classify Confucianism as a religion, as some western scholars have done. The earliest forms of religion were animistic in nature. Later religious ideas were the results of an attempt to deny that death is the end of life. Religions became institutions concerned with human destiny and with experiences of sacredness and ideas of transcendent beings. Some developed the concept of a supernatural being known as God, endowed with spiritual powers capable of controlling the affairs of nature and man. None of these features can be found in the teaching of Confucius. He had no intention of preaching any supernatural power or of founding a religion. 'While you are not able to serve man', he declared, 'how can you serve the spirits? While you do not know life, how can you know death?' His attitude towards religious practices was purely humanistic and pragmatic. 'I sacrifice to the spirits as if they were present', he maintained, 'I sacrifice to the dead as if they were present'. He was quite satisfied to be considered an ordinary human being. He never called himself the Lord or the Light. 'I am not one who was born in possession of knowledge', he told his disciples, 'I am one who is fond of antiquity and who is earnest in seeking knowledge'. His fellow countrymen look upon him as a sage, a teacher and an example of personal cultivation. He has always had a large following but Confucianism has no Messiah, no church and no missionaries. It should be recognised as an ethical teaching or philosophical system rather than as a religion.

THE ORIGIN OF CONFUCIANISM

Confucius was born at a time when the authority of the central Chou government of China, which held sway since 1100 B.C., was declining. During the Chou dynasty the most important political influence in the country was a confederation of states, composed of hundreds of overlordships of varied size and power. The rulers lived in walled cities and felt linked together by cultural heritage rather than by political relations. Clashes were frequent between them and the people outside the cities, who moved about in tribes in the large tracts of grassland in north China and the uncultivated jungles in the south. With the decline of the central Chou government, several powerful states arose which began to expand at the expense of the smaller ones. They struggled against each other for supremacy and wars raged across the land.

Along with this political and social disorder, there was also a break with tradition in the intellectual sphere. A class of merchants and scholars arose who began to rebel against the ancient forms of worship and belief that had largely depended on the feudal system dominated by the king and the lords. As individuals they felt themselves free and independent. The scholars were concerned with the establishment of a new social and political order more than with speculation about an unseen world. Confucius was the first to announce a remedy for the social and political unrest.

Although a commoner by birth Confucius had an opportunity to make a deep study of the Chou cultural heritage while he was employed in the household of the Duke of Lu in modern Shantung. Before his time learning was a monopoly of the ruling families and the possession of knowledge a sign of nobility. He took the classics from the royal household to teach the common people, to anyone regardless of his class or belief. It may be said that he founded the teaching profession in China. His teaching was based on promoting social and political stability through the maintenance of the established power. He sang the praise of the golden age of old, when kind and benevolent rulers graced the throne and peace prevailed throughout the land. He advocated esteem for age over youth, for the past over the present, for the recognised authority over innovation. He was sure that the only way to save the troubled world was by practising loyalty and filial piety. He trained a group of disciples so that his philosophy could be put into practice in case he was given political power. But he could not stem the prevailing tide. He died still a teacher and the chaos and internal strife in the land still continued.

Shortly after Confucius there came another great thinker with a new philosophy, Mo Ti (*c.* 470–391 B.C.). He was an advocate of universal love, devoting himself to the cause of the common people. In his view of society there was no room for the established ceremonies and rituals, which were mere luxury for the nobility. Like Confucius, he travelled widely to preach his gospel and tried to stop the wars raging between the feudal states.

Yang Chu (*c.* 440–362 B.C.) had a different programme to save the warring world. He believed that the fundamental trouble of the world arose from man's ambition, his craving for power and influence. If the individual (or the state) would stop encroaching on the rights of others for his own satisfaction and profit—while at the same time preventing others from robbing or exploiting him—there would be a peaceful world. He held that the universal love as advocated by Mo Ti was idealistic and dangerous. Yang Chu's point of view was essentially individualistic and self-centred.

The teaching of Confucius and the gospel of Mo Ti were blended by Meng-tzu (c. 372–289 B.C.) in his principle of 'kingly government'. He wished to set a limit to the privileges of the feudal class and to provide peaceful living conditions for the common people. A kingly government, he declared, was not a monopoly of the feudal nobility; it should be run by all those who were kind and righteous at heart. Meng-tzu criticised the practice of universal love upheld by Mo Ti and also the individualistic view of Yang Chu. Man, he held, is a social being and cannot be detached from the world in which he lives. Meng-tzu was a champion of the principle that man is good by nature. He was a Confucianist and was solidly behind the principle of filial piety and the integrity of the family system.

At the same time another Confucianist, Hsün-tzu,

stressed the importance of education. He flatly contradicted Meng-tzu's tenet that man is by nature good. Human nature, he argued, is derived from an impersonal, amoral Heaven, and man's emotions and natural desires lead to conflict and therefore are bad. The cure for this situation is education. All men are equal in their innately evil nature, but they are all susceptible to improvement through education. The teacher is all important and therefore to be respected. The process of learning should begin with reciting the classics and end in mastering the *li* rituals and ceremonials which emphasise the proper conduct according to one's status. The classics were considered to furnish a repository of all human wisdom; formal education would improve the nature of man and hence he could live in peace with others according to the prescribed conduct. Hsün-tzu believed in a strict hierarchic order and admired strong discipline in government, advocating that the rulers should control their people by admonitions, proclamations and punishments.

Then came the Taoists, with Lao-tzu (5th century B.C.) and Chuang-tzu (c. 369–286 B.C.) as their leaders. This group of philosophers went so far as to consider that all mental apprehensions were purely relative. There was no such thing as large or small, high or low, right or wrong, long- or short-lived. The only concrete reality was *Tao*, the absolute 'way'. To them the universe was a unity sustained by *Tao* and everything in it was of the same nature. It was Chuang-tzu who has delighted all succeeding generations by his remark that he had dreamt that he was a butterfly fluttering in the sky and after he awoke he could not be sure whether he was still Chuang-tzu who had dreamt that he was a butterfly or actually a butterfly dreaming that he was the philosopher Chuang-tzu. The attitude of the Taoists towards the world was negative and passive. The world was chaotic, so the best way to solve the problem was to get out of it. The Taoists argued for the destruction of all social orders and government organisations and a stop to all moral crusading. 'Action by inaction' was their motto and disinterested non-cooperation became their attitude in life.

This was a period when 'all flowers bloomed and a hundred schools of thought arose'. Some sought to explore the fundamental structure of the universe and they observed in it two forces, the *yin* and the *yang*, one negative and the other positive. The exponent of this school was Tsou Yen (c. 340–260 B.C.), who believed that the inter-action of the two forces gave rise to the five elements or powers—wood, fire, earth, metal and water. These were not only material elements but also the moving power by which the phenomena of the universe were created. To Tsou Yen this explained the structure of nature, of which the human race was but a part. He assumed that there was an interaction between the ways of nature and the affairs of men. He found all kinds of analogies between the natural and the human worlds and came to the conclusion that any manifestations in nature meant that something was about to happen in the human sphere. He also held that proper behaviour on the part of men would influence the way of nature, which he called Heaven. He applied this principle to politics and government, requiring the rulers to do the right things at the right time so that the two worlds might be kept in complete harmony and thus ensure peace on earth.

In the third century B.C. there arose the Legalists, who formulated some practical programmes by which rulers could gain power and unify the country. They felt that human nature was incorrigibly selfish and this inevitably produced conflict. Moralists and champions of the golden age of the past were in fact merely perpetuating the chaotic state of affairs. In a time of upheaval and chaos, the only means to bring about order and security was to introduce severe laws and harsh punishments. Since

45

people are stupidly selfish and ministers untrustworthy self-seekers, the ruler cannot rely on their moral virtues, but must control all alike by clearly defined rewards and punishments. Men should be judged not by their motives, but by their accomplishments. Anyone who fails to achieve what he has been assigned to do must be punished. People should be made responsible for each other's actions and those who fail to denounce a transgressor should be considered guilty of the same crime. If penalties are harsh, the people will be forced into such complete obedience that there will be no need for penalties.

The Legalists also advocated efficient political organisation, the aim of which was to train faithful soldiers and encourage industrious peasants. It was under the emperor Ch'in-shih-huang (246–221 B.C.) that the Legalists' programmes were put into practice and succeeded in unifying the rival states into a gigantic empire. The emperor and his ministers lost no time in enforcing a thorough standardisation of material life, social and political organisation and religious belief. Their drastic measures included the confiscation of all military weapons, the burning of proscribed books and the forced migration of people. In carrying out this programme the emperor meant to build his rule upon such solid foundations that his dynasty would continue for ever. But the people, though longing for peace, were not prepared for such a harsh and cruel regimentation. Rebellion broke out almost as soon as the first emperor died and war and fighting continued for another three years until the country was reunited under the Han dynasty, which lasted for over 400 years (206 B.C.–A.D. 220).

CONFUCIANISM IN PRACTICE

It was the first emperor of this dynasty, Kao-tsu (206–195 B.C.) who allowed the Confucian scholars to put their

46

philosophy into practice. In his younger days he had despised the Confucianists, but when he had conquered the whole nation he found himself confronted with the problem of governing his huge empire. He had won his empire on horseback but he realised he could not govern his people from the back of a horse. Peace and order were essential if he was to keep his throne. He felt he could not adopt the gospel of Mo Ti and practise universal love or share his empire with saintly sages. It was out of the question for an empire builder to abdicate for the good of his people. On the other hand, he could not be as self-centred as Yang Chu had advocated. He had to have regard for the welfare of his subjects. Taoism was also out of the question. Kao-tsu was a man of action and he could not allow his people to retire to a state of passivity as expressed in the philosophy of effortlessness. He was himself in favour of the Legalists. Their philosophy of absolutism and their dictatorial methods were very much to his taste. But the history of the previous dynasty had given him a clear warning. Only fifteen years before, the Legalists had brought the Ch'in dynasty to disaster.

The principles of Confucian government seemed to him to be the most reasonable of all. The Confucian system of ethics was the happy medium; the idea that the ruler should be kind and generous and the subjects filial, loyal and decorous appealed to him. So he allowed the Confucian scholars to put their philosophy into practice. This was based primarily on the concept of the Mandate of Heaven, conceived on a universal scale. As the Son of Heaven, the emperor had received a mandate from above to rule over all the people under the sun. He stood between Heaven above and the people below. He maintained peace and order by doing the right thing at the right time for the people. On the other hand, bad conduct on his part would destroy the sanction he had received and Heaven would readily give its mandate to another man. Such a government was based more on goodness and morality than on political efficiency or economic progress. The Confucian scholars, being educated in the classics, were in a position to advise the emperor on the right conduct and thus assure him of his role in the cosmos. They formulated the principles of a stable universal government and established themselves as an essential part of it.

The Confucian school maintained its dominant position through education. They controlled the educational system by advocating only Confucianism and by repressing or degrading others. Confucian classics with their standard interpretations were taught in schools and universities until they became almost the only literature of the Chinese people. Anyone who wished to acquire education was given a Confucian indoctrination. This became in time the orthodox pattern not only for candidates for government offices, but also for the heirs to the throne, for the tutors of the prince were all Confucian scholars. The world of China was thus united culturally as well as politically and socially. From the Han dynasty onward there was a string of dynasties, some long and some short, some powerful and some weak, and the Son of Heaven might be at times a royal personage or a political adventurer, a monk or a war-lord, a woman or an infant, a bandit or a nomad, but the Confucian teaching and bureaucracy stayed on as the standard form of government. The empire might at times be split into two or more states but there was always one China—a universal China, a Confucian China.

One outstanding and enduring feature of the Confucian system was that it recognised that all people within the four seas are brothers and that the highest ideal for a government is to achieve universal peace. Histories were written by Confucian scholars to assert that all human races were the descendants of the Yellow Emperor. It was held that the Han people in the middle region, the nomads beyond the Great Wall and the tribal minorities scattered over the land were all originally of the same family. Colour, religion, language and class were of little importance so long as one acted on the teaching of the classics which prescribed fair play among all peoples.

NEO-CONFUCIANISM

The fall of the Han dynasty in the third century A.D. was followed by a period of political disunion which lasted for 350 years. Chaos and wars again prevailed. People turned to Taoism for escape and to Buddhism for consolation. The Confucian scholar-officials were obliged to remain in the background, unable to stop the spread of the passivism of the Taoists and the teaching of the Buddhists, which resulted in the abandonment of family life and the rejection of taxation and military service. It was not until the middle of the next dynasty, in the seventh and eighth centuries, that a movement arose to revive the traditional teaching known in the west as Neo-Confucianism. This was far more than just a revival of the ancient heritage. It was a reassessment and revaluation of that heritage in a new climate of opinion, a climate which had been powerfully influenced by Taoism and Buddhism. The scholars were stimulated to fresh thinking in their efforts to redefine man's duties in society and make his moral quest both reasonable and attractive. To them philosophy did not mean the formulation of a theory, but the discovery of the way in which virtue could be best exemplified in life. In their examination and revaluation of the life of Confucius, the ancient teacher was heralded as the example of personal cultivation, a perfect sage, industrious and diligent, wise and righteous, kind and gentlemanly, a model for all men. They declared him 'the most sacred Master', 'the Teacher for all ages'.

Moreover, after delving deep into the teachings of

Taoism and Buddhism, the Neo-Confucianists were unable to free themselves from some of the more acceptable elements in their opponents' ways of life and thinking. Some went so far as to declare that the purpose of the three systems was fundamentally the same and they ought to be united like three rivers flowing into one stream. The working routine of the Confucian system was hard, rigid and formal; now it could be enriched with the simplicity and naturalism of Taoism and the logic and metaphysics of Buddhism. A Chinese could be a Confucianist in office and a Taoist out of it. He could also be privileged to retire to a monastery to discuss the theory of knowledge with the Buddhists. And on the other hand how many Buddhist abbots have become outstanding poets, calligraphers and painters in the Confucian tradition! We may say that Confucianism was reborn with the assistance of these two religions. The Chinese world became greatly enriched by allowing the three to go hand in hand.

THE CHINESE OUTLOOK

Probably more people have lived on the plains of China than on any comparable area on earth. The most significant element in the Chinese landscape is not the land and water or the vegetation and climate but the people. There are human beings everywhere and nowhere else have men been so crowded among their fellows. A Chinese will seldom in all his life have been beyond the earshot of others. This environment has made the Chinese a most social-minded people. The basic thoughts of Confucianism are concerned mainly with human relations, moral values and practical conduct. Throughout the ages it has preached a way of life which is centred on man himself and yet is based on patience and tolerance for others. The Chinese have impressed their own outlook on any culture to which they have been introduced, always reacting in the typical Chinese fashion. This characteristic Chinese attitude and way of life has been variously described as 'the doctrine of the golden mean' or 'happy medium', as 'the spirit of reasonableness' or as 'the religion of common sense'. As this outlook on life, with man at its centre, is Confucian in origin, it seems appropriate to call it 'Confucian Humanism'. Let us see how this philosophy functions in four aspects of human life—the relation of man to Nature, a man's relations with his fellows or the human community, his view of his own self and his attitude towards time and history.

The Chinese regards Nature as comprising three parties. These are Heaven, Man and Earth, with man as the centre. Heaven and earth were created for the benefit of man. Without humanity there would be no reason for the existence of the other two. Enjoying the privilege of being in the centre of the universe, man must play his part by respecting the fatherly heaven and by taking care of the yields of the motherly earth. The traditional Chinese philosophy and science as well as arts and technologies have been developed on this basic assumption.

In man's relations with his fellows, the Chinese classifies the human community into three groups—the crowd, the family and the individual. Confucian Humanism puts the emphasis on the middle group, the family, and most of the Chinese social theories and ethics were concerned to establish the peaceful co-existence of human beings on the family level. The basic principle is the theory of the five human relations, which prescribe the moral obligations between king and minister, father and son, husband and wife, brother and brother and friend and friend. The Confucianists believe that if each person fulfils his duties in his own respective position, the peace and good order of the community will be achieved.

In regard to the individual, human behaviour is considered as exhibiting three temperaments—the aggressive, the restrained and the passive. Most Chinese favour neither aggressiveness nor passivity but prize self-restraint above all else. Children are brought up to be gentle and tolerant towards others. To lose one's temper has always been considered as bad taste and vulgar.

In recognising the three stages in time—past, present and future—the Chinese puts his emphasis on the present, which serves to link the past with the future, making it a continuous process. Thus he has become historical-minded and traditional. In cultural teaching he has insisted on the continuation of the Confucian school of thought. His duty is to inherit the past and pave the way for the future. In the family it is of paramount importance that it should continue for ever. He respects his parents and loves his children. In politics and government he has achieved a continuous history unparalleled in any other people.

The middle course has thus been taken in each of the four spheres we have analysed. Confucian Humanism is a practical philosophy which can be summarised in five fundamental propositions: (*i*) Man is the centre of the universe and therefore human dignity must be upheld. (*ii*) Man is by nature good, not born of sin, and therefore requires no redeemer from heaven. (*iii*) Man has some common sense and he should be able to judge for himself. (*iv*) Any decision made by man ought to be to his own advantage. (*v*) Culture, of which religion and philosophy are but a part, is a tool which man is in a position to use for his own benefit. The Confucian Chinese does not care for any inspiration from high-sounding ideals such as to strive, to seek and to find, to love, to suffer and to sacrifice. He lives not for the Lord of heaven, nor for humanity on earth in general terms, nor for freedom (which is artificial) nor for a higher standard of living (which is relative) but for himself and his parents, sons and grandsons, and for friends whom he learns to care for and respect. Throughout Chinese history the world of the supernatural, the world of nature and the world of men have been considered as bound up in a unity with man as the nucleus. 'All things', proclaims Meng-tzu, the spokesman of Confucianism, 'are complete in me'. And we find the same outlook in Chuang-tzu, the Taoist philosopher, when he says: 'Heaven and earth come into being with me together, and with me all things are one'. The basic concepts of these two widely differing schools of thought, Taoism and Confucianism, are identical, because their outlook is essentially Chinese.

Having defined the fundamental concepts of Confucian Humanism, we may proceed to see how the Chinese have used religion and religious institutions to serve their own purpose.

CHINESE RELIGIOUS BELIEFS

To the superficial observer the Chinese appear very religious. Shrines, temples, monasteries and churches are found in every corner of the country. But we must remember that Confucius refused to have anything to do with the unseen, spiritual or supernatural forces. In his attitude towards spiritual agencies he advised people to respect them but to keep at a distance from them. But the Confucianists never hesitated to adopt any theological ideas that might suit their purpose and as a ruling class they were ready to follow, or to influence the emperor to perform, any kind of worship which would bring benefit to his people, even, on one occasion, the offering of the emperor himself as a sacrifice to heaven in time of serious drought and famine.

Religion in ancient China was animistic in nature. The people paid respects not only to heaven and earth, but also to most natural objects. The worship of rivers and mountains was very popular among the feudal states. Two stories illustrate this. King Chao-wang of Ch'u, of the sixth century B.C., was ill and the diviner told him that the disease was caused by the spirit of the Ho Yellow river, which lay to the north of his domain, and advised that a sacrifice should be offered to this stream. But the king replied: 'The main rivers of my country are Chiang, Han, Huai and Chang and to these I shall offer worship and sacrifice. But Ho is so far away and if I have made mistakes in my rule what right has the god of Ho to interfere?' He did not follow the advice of the diviner and recovered from his illness.

The Confucianists, in propagating the theory of the Mandate of Heaven, advocated that this could be obtained only by a sacrifice offered to Heaven on the summit of the sacred mountain of T'ai-shan (in modern Shangtung) by the emperor himself. When the emperor Ch'in-shih-huang united the whole country in 244 B.C. he was obliged to travel east to perform this important ceremony. Accompanied by seventy Confucian scholars he visited the sacred mountain and prepared to show his people that he was the Son of Heaven. But to his great disappointment the scholars could not agree among themselves on the proper rituals. Some advised that the proceedings should be elaborate, while others insisted on simplicity. At last the emperor found that the best way to solve the problem was to dismiss them all and proceed to perform the sacrifice himself according to the rituals used in his own state in worshipping Heaven. The Confucian scholars were furious. It happened that the emperor's party was stopped half-way up the mountain by rain and storm. The scholars were only too happy to see such a misfortune befall the new emperor and they started a report that he had not obtained the Mandate of Heaven and his dynasty was therefore to be destroyed in no time at all. The emperor was very much disturbed and for revenge he buried many of the scholars alive. His dynasty lasted only fifteen years.

The Chinese also believed in the existence of a spiritual

world in Heaven. The organisation of the sphere above was thought to be similar to that of the stratified structure of human life on earth. The only difference was that in Heaven there was a supreme God who ruled not only his world above, but also the human earth below. An earthly being, when retired to the other sphere, would enjoy the same status as he did in his lifetime. The emperor was recognised as the Son of Heaven and it was altogether fitting that he should worship Heaven. The worship of Heaven functioned as a part of the government. The people thus made no distinction between what is Caesar's and what is God's. Peking, the capital of China for a thousand years, still stands today to show not only the magnificent architecture of this ancient city, but also to symbolise the grandeur of the Son of Heaven and the religious and moral principles underlying the Chinese scheme of things. The seat of government was at the same time the centre of religion.

Some western scholars have called the worship of ancestors the national religion of China. It is indeed the oldest and the most common form of worship, but it can hardly be called a religion. The ancestral spirit is never considered as a god. Because he is a human being, after death his spirit continues to live among his children and takes the same interest in their welfare as he did in his lifetime. If he is a great soul he may protect and guide them in what they undertake. Being of the older genera-tion, the departed spirit needs the reverence and the protection of his descendants through the offerings of food and the burning of paper money. He is to be cared for and served as he was in his old age on earth. The family rela-tionship continues to function in the other sphere. The worship of ancestors is part of the family system.

Confucian Humanism sees the organisation of all human thought and affairs in China in some sort of established order, in which the numbers three and five predominate. This can be illustrated from the philosophical system, the religious pantheon and the list of legendary emperors.

The most popular philosophical speculation about the creation of the universe has been preserved in the *Book of Changes*. According to this ancient system, the most powerful agent in nature is *T'ai-chi*, the supreme ultimate, and from it evolved the two forces *yang* and *yin*, popularly described as male and female, celestial and terrestial, positive and negative. The interplay of these two forces gives birth to the five colours—blue, red, white, black and yellow. Every creature on earth is supposed to have been composed of these five elements in certain proportions.

In religion the same system was at work. It was believed that there were three great gods in the spiritual world— T'ai-yi, the Supreme God, T'ien-yi, the God of Heaven and Ti-yi, the God of Earth. These were assisted by five heavenly kings, named after the five colours. In the second century B.C. the emperor Wu-ti erected an altar in his capital for the worship of all these heavenly deities. The three great gods were enthroned, with T'ai-yi in the centre and the others by his side and the five heavenly kings installed around the altar. After an elaborate ritual and a sacrifice had been performed, the emperor prostrated himself in front of the Supreme God, as his subjects did in front of him. A yellowish vapour appeared in the sky, which indicated that the celestial dignitaries were pleased and there was harmony between heaven and earth, bringing peace, order and prosperity to the land.

In the list of the Chinese emperors in the legendary period there is also a series of three emperors, known as the Supreme Emperor, the Heaven Emperor and the Earth Emperor. They were followed by a series of five emperors, named after the five colours. The best known is the Yellow Emperor, who is considered to be the ancestor of the Chinese people. The trio and quintuplet thus appear in

A Hindu festival.

The statue of Buddha at Nara, Japan.

A buddhist
at prayer.

The main building of the Grand Shinto Shrine at Ise.

A Shinto wedding ceremony.

The Mosque of Omar in Jerusalem.

Inside a
Muslim tomb.

The Golden Temple at Amritsar.

philosophy, in religion and in history. All the three systems have been influenced by the basic Chinese conception that all things are one, all employing the same general scheme of thinking.

To the Chinese, religion is a part of life and people should be free to worship in whatever way they prefer. The variety of religious cults throughout the land seems endless. The worship of heaven and earth, mountain and tree, river and sea, door and hearth and many other kinds of objects was common. The ancestor was venerated in the form of a wooden tablet, in the shape of an image made of clay, wood, ivory, stone, silver or gold. Others were represented in pictures drawn or simply names inscribed on paper, silk, lacquer or porcelain. There has been no problem of the proper place for the performance of religious worship. Shrines and temples may be erected anywhere—in the city, on the mountain top, along a river, on the roadside, in front of a door, provided the place is convenient for the worshipper.

Religions in some other countries tend to become exclusive and even aggressive. The followers must try to convert others to their own faith. This does not seem applicable to the Chinese. They are probably the only people who have deliberately tried to unite several distinct religious systems of thought—especially the leading ones of Confucianism, Taoism and Buddhism—into one system. The Chinese who have been brought up in an atmosphere of patience and tolerance recognise no religious barriers. All religions are but tools of life and should fit into the Chinese scheme of things.

The man-centred attitude of the Chinese towards religion may be illustrated by the way they used to treat their city gods, the object of one of the most popular cults in old China. The city temple was always a very busy centre for entertainment and other social gatherings. The god of the city was neither commissioned by Heaven nor appointed by the government, but invited by the people themselves. The candidate selected was usually the spirit of a famous man who had performed some spectacular achievements in his lifetime. An image was then made to look like the chosen hero, an auspicious day was picked and his spirit was invited to reside in the idol, which was enthroned in the temple. The god was commissioned to look after the spiritual welfare of the city, in much the same way as the mayor would govern the public life of the people. The god was expected to do his best for them.

It might happen that there was a drought in the district. The river dried up and the water in the wells was getting low. The people and the officials offered sacrifice to Heaven and prayed for rain. They dressed a couple of young men as a dragon representing the god of Rain and subjected them to water splashing and teasing of various kinds. This was a very old tradition. For a period they would close the butchers' shops, following the Buddhist practice and refraining from eating pork. If all these measures failed to produce rain, they would go to pray to their city god. He was offered a luxurious sacrifice and promised every conceivable reward and honour. If nothing happened, he would be regarded as indifferent to the welfare of the people. He would be removed from his comfortable throne and left naked in the sun to taste the heat of its rays. If there was still no rain, the city god would suffer a severe flogging. He would finally be dismissed and burnt in a fire and the soul of another famous man of the past would be invited to take his place. This was the way the man-centred Chinese treated their gods. If they were useless to man, they might just as well be sent to where they belonged.

In the Chinese culture religious beliefs and practices

functioned mainly as part of social behaviour. The country has been opened to many religions from outside. Buddhism, Hinduism, Zoroastrianism, Manism, Islam, Lamaism and Christianity have all had their opportunities. A foreign religion would have to adapt itself to fit into the Chinese scheme before it could take root and flourish. Buddhism furnishes a good example. This religion was introduced into China in the first century A.D. It took several centuries to become properly organised and to exert its influence in practically every branch of Chinese life. Buddhism has rendered some valuable service to China. The true Buddhist is a kind person, more pacific and more philanthropic than others. Buddhism inspires him to be kind to the passing stranger, who receives no attention in the Confucian system of relations between man and man. The exacting routine of life is made easier by observing Buddhist customs. The fair in the temple, the pilgrimage to the sacred mountain, the enjoyment of the vegetarian dinner and many other functions serve to enlighten the life of the people.

Buddhist monasteries are ready to admit a Confucian scholar to live in Buddhist retirement without becoming a monk or even professing the religion. A Christian church might not tolerate a Buddhist monk preaching from its pulpit, but a Buddhist abbot would readily allow a Christian conference to be held in his monastery and the monks would entertain the Christian members as cheerfully as they would entertain the Confucian scholars. Buddhism has been used by the Chinese in much the same way as they use other elements of their culture. The religion is accepted because it has become Chinese. In itself Buddhism is fundamentally an escape from the earthly world, which Buddha believed to be painful. But the Chinese, with their tradition of Confucian Humanism, have transformed it into a social institution and reinstated it among worldly affairs. The Chinese Buddhists are cheerful fellows and they enjoy life as much as other men. Whether their attitude is logical or not is of no importance. To become Chinese, it must be reasonable.

The procedure at a Chinese funeral is a very good example to show the way in which people employ all religions to serve their own purpose. At the last stage of a man's life in China he is assisted by all religions. Taoist priests and Buddhist monks are invited to usher his soul into their respective paradises and to take part in the funeral procession. At the end of the column a Confucian scholar in a sedan chair travels with them to the cemetery, from which he is supposed to bring home the soul of the deceased in a tablet for the ancestral hall. If a Christian minister were willing to co-operate, he might have been invited to say a prayer before the coffin is lowered into the grave.

Similarly, it was common for a temple to be shared by Buddhist monks, Taoist priests and Confucian school teachers at the same time. To the Chinese who base their judgment on practical common sense the gods of a religion are of comparatively little importance; the test is whether a religion is useful to men as part of their life. The judgment rests with man himself.

CHINA TODAY

It will be seen from this survey that the China of the present is the product of a long development, a continuous record of more than three thousand years. There has always been one China—a universal China, a Confucian China. There has been many a time in its history when some religious or political system favoured by the rulers has forced the Confucianists into a secondary role. But Confucianism seems to be quite familiar with the tactics of subduing a powerful opponent by joining forces with it and making use of its services. During this present century China has been compelled by various forces to change from a universal to a nationalistic China. This process began with the revolution of 1911, which dethroned the emperor, and has culminated in the present state of the country as the People's Republic of China. In such a revolution and under the Communist regime, religious beliefs and practices such as have been described here would appear to have no part to play. For the present, Maoism seems to be the 'religion' by which China is to be reshaped in order to take her place as a member of the modern world. All other religions have had to accept this state of affairs or else have been eliminated. This may be regarded as a logical development of the historical process and quite in keeping with the practical outlook of the Chinese people.

FOR FURTHER READING:

B. S. Bonsall: *Confucianism and Taoism* (Epworth Press).
Chan, Wing-Tsit: *Religious Trends in Modern China* (O.U.P.)
H. G. Creel: *Chinese Thought from Confucius to Mao Tse-Tung* (Eyre and Spottiswode).
Lin Yutang (editor): *The Wisdom of China* (Joseph).
Liu Wu-Chi: *Confucius* (Allen and Unwin).
A. Waley: *Three Ways of Thought in Ancient China* (Allen and Unwin).

FOR INFORMATION:

Dr. Joseph Needham, Gonville and Caius College, Cambridge.

4

The Shintoists

The word Shinto means 'the way of the gods'. The name was given to the religion, which was observed throughout Japan in early times, in order to distinguish it from Buddhism, which began to spread in that country in the sixth century A.D. Shintoism did not have its origin in any individual person or historical event, but arose from the veneration of the forces of nature and spirits which is characteristic of primitive peoples. The early devotees of this religion saw almost everything as an object of worship, as containing or revealing the presence of a god or spirit —mountains, rivers, unusual trees, rocks and stones.

The people erected shrines, which were originally simple shelters to protect the worshippers from the elements and in some cases no doubt to protect the object of worship also. Gradually the shrines developed from these simple protective structures to the more elaborate buildings which can be seen in any town or village in Japan today. They are approached through a *torii* or entrance gate and consist usually of a main sanctuary, into which only the priest may enter, with an oratory or open prayer hall for the worshippers near by. Some of the shrines are very old, but there is often a difference between the age of the shrine itself and the date of its foundation.

The actual building may have been repaired and even rebuilt many times, for nearly all Japanese shrines are made of wood, while its foundation may date back a thousand years. The most famous of these is the Grand Shrine of Ise, the most sacred spot in all Japan, dedicated to Amaterasu the Sun goddess.

Objects of worship may include almost anything, ranging from Mount Fuji, which towers 12,000 feet in central southern Japan, the most venerated among the sacred mountains, to the ancient imperial insignia of a mirror, a sword and a jewel, with which, according to the Japanese myth, the first emperor was invested by the Sun goddess, from whom he was descended. These and other objects, together with statues of Amaterasu, are found in shrines throughout Japan and are examples of what are called *shintai* or 'God-bodies'—objects which are themselves the abode of a god. A round stone is a very common *shintai*. There are other objects which are not entitled to veneration in themselves but may be worshipped because a deity may be invoked to dwell in them. These are called *mitamashira* or 'substitute spirits'. These sacred objects may be desposited in a shrine, usually in a sealed receptacle, the contents of which may be unknown even to the priests in charge of the shrine.

Religions which have their origin in animism (the belief in spirits everywhere) are not usually exclusive and this is certainly the case with Shinto. From Buddhism, which spread to Japan by way of China, there came foreign gods and rituals, more elaborate shrines and ideas of astrology and divination. From Taoism and other Chinese religions, Shintoists took the practices of magic, sorcery and fortune-telling and they cultivated asceticism. Contact with Confucianism introduced ancestor-worship and provided Shinto with a system of ethics.

The same may be said of the myths of Shinto—stories about the gods and the creation of the world. Some of

63

these are primitive, but in most cases they have come under foreign influences and owe much to Buddhist and Chinese ideas. The Shinto gods seem to have been in the beginning local deities, manifested in natural phenomena. The Sun goddess came into prominence in the early period of Shinto. The shrine at Ise is especially dedicated to her and she is worshipped also in many other prominent and local shrines. She may be regarded as supreme, but there are many other gods.

Shinto has developed a system of priesthood and there are school and university facilities for the training of priests. The priesthood is organised on a graded basis, with chief priests at the top and 'conductors', who officiate at the local shrines, at the bottom. The emperor was ranked among the first grades of the priesthood and was often depicted on formal occasions in the robes of a chief priest.

This brings us to the question of the relation between Shinto and the state. The Sun goddess Amaterasu was regarded as the ancestress of the powerful Yamato clan, who established their capital in the centre of Japan in the sixth century B.C. The first emperor was said to be directly descended from her and succeeding emperors were thus worshipped as divine. There is nothing novel about deifying rulers. With primitive peoples this seems to have been a natural tendency and the practice was also common in ancient times in the civilisations of the Middle East, whence it spread to Europe in the time of the Roman empire. In Japan it became a matter of deliberate policy, in order to strengthen the position of the state. About 1868 there began a period of national growth and expansion and Shinto was used to provide the spiritual impetus for this. The Sun goddess already enjoyed wide popularity and the divine status of the emperor was emphasised, so that he was worshipped along with the gods at centres like the shrine at Ise.

This veneration for the emperor became a matter of state policy. Only a simple act of worship was required and this was declared by the authorities to be non-religious, so some Christians and adherents of other religions felt free to offer this without qualms of conscience. Along with this worship of the emperor went state support of Shinto, which became something like an established church. Not only were the salaries of the priests paid, shrines kept in repair and various grades of priests appointed by the state but the government also exercised control over the ideas of Shinto. For a brief period prior to and during the Second World War, Shinto became very nationalistic and intolerant. But after the defeat of Japan in 1945 and its occupation by American forces, Shinto was removed from state control. The emperor himself declared that he was not divine and he is no longer worshipped as a descendant of the gods. Many small shrines declined because of lack of financial support, but great numbers still exist and are supported by the gifts of Shinto adherents.

There are a number of Shinto 'sects', religious societies which emphasise one aspect of their religion, although the ideas of some of them have only a slight connection with Shinto. They are often of peasant origin. Many of them have some kind of faith-healing ministry. They flourish because they make a personal appeal to their followers. One of them, Tenri-kyo, has well over a million adherents. The name means 'the Teaching of the Heavenly Reason' and the sect was founded in 1838 by a woman named Miki, of Yamato, who claimed that she was possessed by a god who called himself the Lord of Heaven.

Shinto has no formal creed or statement of faith but there are books which could be regarded as sacred scriptures, such as the 'Chronicle of Ancient Events' (*Kojiki*), which sets forth the stories of the origin of the gods and the beginnings of mankind, with the aim of demonstrating the divine origin of the ruling family and the state. It was compiled in A.D. 712 at the command of the reigning emperor. Another book is 'The Chronicles of Japan' (*Nihongi*), compiled in A.D. 720, which contains alternative versions of the myths and events recorded in the *Kojiki*.

In spite of its primitive origins, Shinto has proved to be remarkably persistent. It still preserves a good deal of its original character and is very much part of the way of life of modern Japan. It exercises a deep influence on the lives of the people from beginning to end. At the birth of a child, the usual custom is to register the baby at the family shrine. The children are also taken to the shrine during their third, fifth and seventh years. These are festive occasions, when the children are dressed in bright kimonos. Marriages usually take place at a Shinto shrine, with the priest officiating, and many shrines have large, pleasant halls attached where the wedding reception can take place. Burials, on the other hand, are frequently taken by a Buddhist priest and for this occasion the mourning family visit the local Buddhist temple. Shinto shrines are also visited by individuals for personal devotion. The worshipper must be free from disease and will take care to see that he is purified by rinsing the mouth and performing special ceremonial washing before entering the shrine. The worship is of a very simple nature. The worshipper bows before and after making his offering, then claps his hands before proceeding on his way. To clap the hands was in ancient Japan a general sign of respect, but became confined to religious worship.

In addition to visiting the shrines for worship or for advice, many people have a small shrine in their homes. This is sometimes called a God-shelf and strict Shintoists will make their devotions before it at the beginning of the day or before visiting a shrine. These devotions are brief, often consisting merely of making a bow, then a pause for reflection which is followed by a clap of the hands and the worshipper moves on.

In addition to ceremonies connected with birth, marriage and life in the home, Shinto is also in evidence in many other spheres. The ground on which a house is to be built is often blessed by a Shinto priest and when the building is finished it is subject to Shinto purification rites. Even the day on which people take up residence in a house is determined by the religious authorities. There are many other situations in which religious rites are required and priests are consulted. Purification is a notable feature of the religion; this may explain why Japanese people are so concerned about bodily cleanliness and health.

Shinto, as an animistic religion, was originally concerned mainly with ceremonies and the correct approach to the gods, rather than with conduct and morality. In this sphere Japan has been influenced by Confucian ideas such as the reverence due to one's ancestors. This makes a difference to the way in which children treat their parents, both in early and in later life. The Confucian ideals of conduct have shown themselves in the correct attitude of children towards parents, of the citizens towards the emperor, of the workers towards their work. Thus Shinto, although modified in the course of many centuries, still exercises a profound influence upon almost every aspect of life among its adherents.

FOR FURTHER READING:

M. Anesaki: *History of Japanese Religion* (Routledge).
R. Hammer: *Japan's Religious Ferment* (S.C.M.).
D. C. Holtom: *The National Faith of Japan* (Routledge).
A. C. Underwood: *Shintoism* (Epworth Press).

P. Wheeler: *Sacred Scriptures of the Japanese* (Allen and Unwin).

FOR INFORMATION:

Father A. Snell, Kobe Shudoin, 1–304 Iguchi-ga-hira, Tamon-Cho, Tarumi, Kobe 655, Japan.

5

The Jews

The Jews constitute one of the smallest of the religious groups mentioned in this book, but the influence of their writings and their teachings has been crucial in the development of Western European civilisation and the Jews have carried their faith to practically every corner of the globe. Judaism—the religion of the Jewish people— has given birth to two daughter religions, Christianity and Islam, yet it has retained its own specific individuality and continued to be a dynamic force for its adherents.

How have the Jews managed to preserve their identity despite their small numbers and the many forces, both direct and indirect, that have threatened to destroy them? We shall see that the answer to this question involves us in a close study both of the history of the Jewish people and of the principles and practices of their faith. This com- bination of history and faith is, in fact, the first aspect of the problem which we must deal with, because, when we discuss the Jewish people, we shall find that in nature and character they are unlike other peoples. We cannot really say that the Jews are a race, because members of a race are distinguished as such by the fact that they all have physical characteristics in common, whereas Jews are of many different physical types. There are tall, fair Jews, and short, dark Jews. There are Jews of a Chinese or Indian appearance. And some say that the black Falashas of Ethiopia are also of Jewish origin. On the other hand, the early Hebrews certainly did belong to the Semitic race, and still to-day a Jew, unless he is a convert from another religion (or from none), is a Jew primarily because he was born of Jewish parents. However, it is clear that during their long history the Jews have mixed and married with other peoples, and so there is hardly a trace today of 'pure' Jewish descent.

Nor can it be said that the Jews today are a nation. The Hebrews at the time of King David and King Solomon were a nation, and the Israelis in our own time are also a nation. But most Jews today do not live in Israel. They are nationals of other countries, of the United Kingdom, of the United States, of France, of Argentina, of the Soviet Union, and so on. On the other hand they have in common certain national characteristics. They have a common history, and also a language, Hebrew, which acts as a unifying influence, although most Jews cannot speak it fluently.

They also have a common religion, Judaism. And this has been a unifying factor among all Jews from the earliest period of their history down to comparatively recent times. The physical focus of Jewish communal life has been the synagogue, and, preceding that, the Temple in Jerusalem. But here again we must admit that not all Jews today are faithful to their religion. Some Jews profess themselves to be atheists, but would nevertheless not dream of abandoning the name 'Jew' or of being 'unfaithful' to the Jewish people. So we see that it is extremely difficult to arrive at a satisfactory definition of the term 'Jew'. So difficult is it, in fact, that a recent Prime Minister of Israel, David Ben-Gurion, sent out a questionnaire to Jewish scholars all over the world asking them to state what in their view a Jew was, and the replies that came back varied in the emphases they placed on the racial, national, and religious characteristics of the Jewish people. Perhaps we must be content simply to note the various ingredients that go to make up the Jewish people, and then go on to examine the specifically religious elements that have been so much a part of Jewish experience, and that have to such a large extent made the Jew what he is today.

THE ORIGIN OF JUDAISM

The Jews trace their origin back to the Exodus from Egypt, an event which is described in some detail in the Bible, and which modern scholars date roughly in the thirteenth century B.C. The Bible also tells us of the patriarchal ancestors of these Hebrews who were enslaved in Egypt and then later freed. We read of Abraham, Isaac and Jacob who, according to Jewish tradition, were the first men to recognise the one God, and who tried to persuade others to renounce paganism and idolatry. But the Hebrews as a people did not become conscious of their divine mission until their release from Egyptian bondage and their subsequent experience of a revelation of God at Mount Sinai in the desert. This event, described in chapters 19 and 20 of the Book of Exodus, set the seal on the whole future development of the Jewish people and their religion. We cannot know what actually took place at Mount Sinai so many centuries ago. But we can be sure that that experience was so fundamental and profound that Jewish religious leaders always pointed back to it as the beginning of the 'covenant' relationship that existed between God and the Jewish people. Through Moses, who acted both as political head of the Hebrews in Egypt and also as spiritual intermediary between them and God at Sinai, the Hebrews accepted a divine law which imposed upon them certain grave ethical and ritual responsibilities. This was the essence of the 'covenant' that was made between God and the Hebrews—a joint agreement, as it were, which promised divine protection in return for human obedience.

The Ten Commandments have become recognised as the very heart of this agreement, and their simple and basic ethical precepts may be regarded perhaps as the greatest contribution that Jewish moral idealism has made to human civilisation. But it should be remembered that the whole of the Pentateuch (the Five Books of Moses) was regarded by Jewish tradition as a divine gift to Moses at Sinai, and all Jewish religious theory and practice was eventually derived from it.

Our main source for the early history of the Jewish people is of course the Bible, and much of its evidence has been corroborated by archaeological discovery. The Bible, which for the Jews contains the Hebrew Scriptures commonly known as the Old Testament (and excludes the Apocrypha and New Testament), was written by a number of men over a long period of time (c. 1200 B.C.–150 B.C.). It is really a collection of books (which is what the Greek word *biblia* means) and deals with ethics, law, theology, history, prayer, ritual and many other things. But there is one theme which underlies practically the whole collection—the attempt to discover how God wishes man to live, with all the associated questions concerning the nature of God and man, and the detailed requirements of religious ritual and ethical practice.

In Biblical times the moral ideals of the Hebrews were already extremely advanced. Despite the barbarous, and often very primitive, times in which they lived (reflections of which can be discovered in the Bible itself) the Hebrews had already perceived that it was essential to protect another person's property, to administer justice fairly without favouring the rich or oppressing the poor, to treat a stranger equitably and hospitably, and to love one's neighbour as oneself (*Leviticus*, 19.18). Time and again, whenever the people fell short of these ideals great religious preachers arose, who castigated them for their failings, and reminded them of the covenant that their forbears had made with God. These spokesmen were the prophets, the foremost of whom were Amos, Isaiah, Jeremiah, Ezekiel and the 'Isaiah' of the Babylonian exile. They spoke in the name of God and were not afraid to stand up in the presence of the Kings of Judah and Israel, and risk their lives in the cause of truth and righteousness. The writings of these men still have a deep and relevant meaning for us today. It is to them that we owe the association of ethics and moral conduct with religion, which we are inclined to take for granted today. One of the prophets summed up his message in these words: 'God has told you what is good; and what does the Lord require of you but to do justice and to love mercy and kindness and to walk humbly with your God?' (*Micah*, 6.8).

In other respects, however, the religion of the Hebrews in Biblical times was very different from that of the Jews today. Like all the other peoples of the ancient Near East they believed that the proper way to worship God was to make an offering of grain, fruit or animal sacrifice, and this was done regularly by the priests, first of all in the portable sanctuary called the tabernacle and then, after the time of King Solomon, in the Temple in Jerusalem. There were special offerings for the Sabbath and Festivals, and others were brought by people seeking atonement for sin, or by women as a thanksgiving after childbirth, and so on. In all cases, however, only the priests were permitted to make the actual presentation of the offering on the altar.

A great transformation took place in the history both of the Jews and of Judaism in the year 70 A.D. In that year the Temple in Jerusalem was destroyed by the Romans, and, since sacrifices could according to the tradition be offered in no other place, the sacrificial system came to an end, and the priests to all intents and purposes lost their religious function. This was not the first time that the Jews had suffered political repression and religious persecution. The Northern Kingdom of Israel had been destroyed by the Assyrians in 721 B.C. In 586 B.C. the Babylonians had deported hundreds of leading Jewish families and destroyed the first temple, which was rebuilt some 70 years later. A Greek-Syrian king had tried to stamp out the Jewish religion in 168 B.C. but was defeated by the Maccabees. And so devastation, this time by the Romans, was not something to which Jews were unaccustomed. But on this occasion it brought with it far greater changes. A new type of religious leader arose in the Jewish community. He was called *rabbi*, which means literally 'my teacher', and Jewish spiritual leaders still bear that title. Rabbis had existed for decades before the destruction of the Temple, but after 70 A.D., with the priestly hierarchy gone, they really came into their own. They may justly be called the architects of Judaism, for they managed with great skill to transform the Hebraism of the Bible into the Judaism of a later age. This they did by studying the Bible and its religious traditions with great diligence, discussing it endlessly among themselves, and teaching it to their followers in the synagogues—places of assembly, learning and prayer, which had gradually grown up wherever Jews lived in any numbers together.

The rabbis realised that it was not sufficient to teach religion in only general terms. So they endeavoured to make of Judaism a very precise way of life in which practically every act was carried out in the light of some religious precept or other. A vast rabbinic literature was written on matters of Jewish law. A code, called the *Mishnah*, was put together in the year A.D. 200, and this, after centuries of study and commentary, was reproduced (c. 500 A.D.) in a much enlarged form as the *Talmud*. In addition to this the homiletical parables and sermons of the rabbis were collected, and these contain many beautiful stories, legends and biblical interpretations. So we have a vast treasure-house of Jewish wisdom, which has been an inspiration, second only to the Bible itself, to all succeeding generations of Jews. Indeed the name *Torah* (Instruction) is applied both to the Pentateuch and to the body of rabbinic teaching which followed it.

So by the early Middle Ages the foundations of the Judaism we know today had been firmly laid although, as the centuries passed, changes continued to be made both in thought and practice.

THE BELIEFS OF THE JEWS

Jews believe in the existence of one supreme deity who is both creator and master of the universe, and at the same time concerned with the lives of individuals on earth. So he is in one respect remote from man, and not completely comprehensible to him, and, in another, very near to man, in that spiritual communication is possible between them through prayer, meditation, religious experience and observance. The task of the Jew is to seek continually to know God's will and to endeavour to carry it out in the world, as far as it is possible for him to do so. The major and overriding purpose of his life is to work for a period of peace between man and man, when 'the Kingdom of God will be established on earth'. Subservient to this great ideal, the ideal of the messianic age, are all the many commandments (*mitzvot*) which the Jew is obliged to observe throughout his daily life, and those commandments are traditionally thought to have been imposed upon, and willingly accepted by, the Jewish people during the revelation at Sinai.

Man is a free agent and is at liberty to accept or to reject the 'yoke' of the commandments. He is in control of his own life, and is not subject to the arbitrary dictates of any superhuman power. Man is neither wholly evil nor wholly good, but is composed of both an evil and a good inclination. By agreeing to follow the commandments of his God, he can himself overcome his own evil impulses. The Jew's task is to sanctify the whole of his own personal life and the life of the world. God made the body as well as the spirit, and there is not in Judaism that strict division between the material and the spiritual world which we may discern in some other faiths. The physical pleasures of life should also be considered sacred, and it is possible 'to hallow the name of God' through all our acts.

In the task of world redemption the Jews believe that they have a particular role. They consider themselves to be 'the servants of the Lord', but this does not imply any undue favouritism on God's part. On the contrary, it involves them in a special responsibility towards God and his teachings, which may bring upon them the misunderstanding and frequently the hostility of other peoples.

JEWISH RELIGIOUS PRACTICES

Study of the *Torah* and practice of it are the twin poles on which Judaism revolves. The Jew must be educated in Judaism before he is capable of fulfilling its requirements, and so learning has always been stressed and admired in the Jewish community. The main centre of Jewish practice and Jewish commitment is the Jewish home and family. This has been a major factor in the preservation and survival of Judaism. Every Sabbath and every festival is celebrated in some form in the home, and in most cases the home ritual and observance is of equal importance with that of the synagogue, and may indeed be considered to be of greater importance.

The Jewish Sabbath (*Shabbat*, a Hebrew word meaning 'rest') begins on the Friday evening at dusk and continues until dusk on the Saturday. The lady of the house lights the Sabbath candles to institute the day of rest, and the head of the family recites the *kiddush*, which is a prayer of sanctification of the Sabbath, said (or chanted) over a cup of wine. Another blessing is said, over bread, and a special festive Sabbath meal is eaten. The main service at the synagogue takes place on Saturday morning, when daily prayers are supplemented by special prayers for the Sabbath, and where passages from the scroll of the law (the *Sefer Torah*), which contains the Pentateuch in its original Hebrew form, are read, to be followed by an additional section (*haftarah*) from the Prophets. The Sabbath is concluded by another ceremony in the home called *havdalah* (division) in which a lighted candle is extinguished in wine to symbolise the end of the day, and a spice-box is handed round the family so that they may savour the sweetness of the Sabbath as it departs. Orthodox Jews refrain from doing any work on the Sabbath so that it may be a complete day of rest, as the Bible itself commanded.

Apart from the Sabbath, the two most holy days of the Jewish calendar are the New Year (*Rosh ha-Shnaha*), and the Day of Atonement (*Yom Kippur*, more properly *Yom ha-Kippurim*). The Jewish calendar is lunar, and each month consists of either 28 or 29 days. In order to synchronise this with the solar calendar, a leap year is necessary from time to time, in which an extra month is added. The New Year is celebrated on the first day of the Hebrew month, *Tishri*, which occurs in the autumn. In the Bible it is called a 'Day of Memorial', and a 'Day of the Blowing of Trumpets'. This gives the key-note to the festival, whose theme is the enthronement of God as King of the universe, and it serves to remind the Jews of their sacred covenant obligations. A very ancient form of trumpet, a ram's horn (*shofar*), is blown in the synagogue, and its piercing tones impress the solemnity of the occassion upon the worshippers. The New Year's day institutes a ten-day period of penitence, culminating in the Day of Atonement, when Jews, during a day-long synagogue ritual, confess their sins both as individuals and as a community. This whole day is spent in fasting as a sign of repentance. One of the features of the service is the reading of the Book of Jonah in the afternoon.

The Jewish calendar also contains three so-called Pilgrimage Festivals, in Spring, Summer and Autumn. These are Passover (*Pesach*), Weeks (*Shavuot*) and Tabernacles (*Sukkot*). On these three occasions, when the Temple was still standing, the Jew was expected to make his pilgrimage to Jerusalem in order to make a special festive offering. These three festivals also have in common the fact that they were originally ancient Canaanite agricultural festivals which were adapted by the Hebrews and invested with an additional historical significance.

Passover, a seven-day festival, was a celebration of the barley harvest, but it became associated specifically with the Exodus from Egypt, as its other name, 'the season of our freedom', clearly demonstrates. During this festival no leaven is used, because the story has it that the Jews had to leave Egypt in such haste that their dough did not have time to rise before it was baked. So Jews eat *matzah* (unleavened bread). On the first night of the festival a special meal is eaten in the home. This is called the *Seder* (order), and the purpose of it is to re-create, as it were, in one's own home the Exodus from Egypt. Special symbolic foods are arrayed on the table, and the children of the family ask set questions about the proceedings, so that, in reply, the head of the household has an opportunity to recount the story of the Exodus. A special prayer-book called *Haggadah* (Narration) is used, and it is often profusely illustrated in order to hold the attention of the children.

Passover is followed some seven weeks later by the Festival of Weeks, also called Pentecost. This is a one-day festival, and marks the wheat harvest, but more important, it also commemorates the revelation of the *Torah* by God to Moses at Mount Sinai, and so it is also called 'the season of the giving of our *Torah*'.

The third of the Pilgrimage Festivals is the eight-day festival of Tabernacles. Originally an occasion for celebrating the in-gathering of the fruit-harvest, it came to be associated with the bounty of God in general and particularly in connection with the lives of the Hebrews during their wandering in the wilderness. Just as at Passover Jewish families try to re-create the Exodus, so here an attempt is made to re-experience the type of precarious life that the ancient Hebrews led. A frail shelter of some kind (*Sukkah*) is constructed by the family, and during the period of the festival this is traditionally regarded as one's home, especially at meal-times. The ritual in the synagogue is distinguished by the carrying of the 'four kinds' (*Arba Minim*) of vegetation mentioned in the Bible, according to rabbinic interpretation. These are the date-palm, the myrtle, the willow and the citron.

The festival of Tabernacles is followed immediately by the Rejoicing in the Torah (*Simchat Torah*), which marks the end of one annual cycle of readings from the Pentateuch, and the beginning of another cycle. The scrolls of the *Torah* are carried in procession round the synagogue, and often out into the streets as well, accompanied by singing, dancing, and considerable gaiety.

On the Feast of Lots (*Purim*) the Jews commemorate the deliverance of Persian Jewry from the extermination planned by King Ahasuerus and his vizier, Haman, as described in the Book of Esther. And the eight-day Festival of Dedication (*Chanukkah*) celebrates the great victory of the Maccabees over the Syrians in the year 165 B.C. It is marked by the lighting at home of an eight-branched candelabrum (*menorah*), every evening of the festival.

It will be clear from the foregoing account how much of Jewish festival observance is practised in the home. And the Jewish character of the family is even more emphasised by the observance of the dietary laws (*kashrut*), which are derived from the Bible, and which were elaborated by the rabbis in great detail. Only certain kinds of meat, fish and fowl may be eaten. Animals for food must be slaughtered in a particular way, and there must be no mixing of milk with meat. These laws are still adhered to by large numbers of Jews, although there is evidence that there has been some decline in the strictness of their observance in the Jewish population as a whole.

Prayers in both synagogue and home are recited in Hebrew, and since many of the prayers are taken directly from the Bible, in particular the Psalms, Hebrew must be one of the oldest languages still spoken today in an unchanged form. (The modern Hebrew spoken in Israel has, of course, undergone considerable changes since biblical times). Orthodox Jews pray three times daily, and the Jews' basic prayer is the affirmation of the unity of God, known as the *Shema*, taken from *Deuteronomy*, 6.4: 'Hear, O Israel: the Lord our God is one Lord: and and thou shalt love the Lord thy God with all thine heart and with all thy soul and with all thy might'. The passage goes on to urge that these words should be impressed on the heart and should always be before the eyes and in the homes of the Jew. These precepts are taken literally and little boxes (*tefillin*) containing the *Shema* (the Hebrew for the opening word 'Hear') are worn between the eyes and on the arm nearest the heart during morning prayer; a small receptacle (*mezuzah*) containing the same prayer is permanently affixed to the door-posts of the house.

Every stage of the life of the Jew is marked by a specifically religious act. A male child is circumcised at the age of eight days in accordance with an ancient Hebrew practice first mentioned in connection with Abraham and his sons. Synagogues provide Jewish education for children from the age of six or seven upwards, and there are also in Britain a number of full-time Jewish day-schools. At the age of 13 a boy becomes *bar-mitzvah* (son of the command-ment) when traditionally he becomes fully responsible for his own religious acts. This occasion is marked by his being summoned to the reading of the Torah in the synagogue. Jewish marriage is solemnised beneath a canopy (*chuppah*) which symbolises the couple's first home, and also the presence of God which shelters them. The bridegroom gives the bride a ring and declares: 'Behold, you are consecrated to me by this ring according to the law of Moses and Israel'. They then share a cup of wine. Jewish marriage is in essence a legal contract, attested by witnesses. And there is provision for divorce if the marriage breaks down, although strenuous attempts are usually made to preserve the marriage if possible. Divorced persons may contract another marriage in the synagogue.

Mourning customs among Jews are extremely detailed. The overriding concern is that the bereaved should be comforted and consoled by relations and friends. After the burial (orthodox Jews do not allow cremation) a strict seven-day period of mourning ensues called *shivah* (seven) when the bereaved remain at home, and are visited by all who wish to condole with them. Services are held at the home on each evening, while the bereaved sit on low stools as a sign of mourning. A less intense period of mourn-ing follows for the next eleven months, after which a memorial stone to the deceased is usually consecrated.

In all these activities the rabbi plays an important part. But it should be realised that he is essentially a layman, specially skilled in Jewish law and tradition, whose advice and help are valued. He does not carry out priestly functions; he has no special intermediary power between man and God. Judaism is a democratic religion without any priestly hierarchy. All Jews have the obligation to study and practise their religion, and practically all the functions of the rabbi may be carried out by any Jew who has the necessary knowledge and expertise. The rabbi is primarily a teacher. The synagogue where he works is a social and educational centre as well as a house of worship, but, of course, the most respected part of the building is the place of prayer. The focal point here is the Holy Ark (*Aron ha-kodesh*) situated along the wall that faces Jerusalem. It is really nothing more than a cupboard, or a niche in the wall, that contains the scrolls of the Torah. These scrolls are made of parchment and the Pentateuch is written on them by hand in Hebrew. The scrolls are often decorated with beautiful mantles, bells and breast-plates, and the Ark is usually curtained or screened off from the main body of the synagogue. In front of the Ark hangs the Perpetual Light (*Ner Tamid*), an oil lamp which is always alight, and which symbolises the altar-fire which was continually burning in the Temple Court in days of old. The service is conducted by the reader or cantor from a raised platform in front of the Ark called the *almemar* or *bimah*. It is usual for men to wear some kind of hat or skull-cap in the synagogue and indeed strictly orthodox Jews never go bareheaded. In traditional synagogues men and women sit separately. Because of the Jewish reluctance to transgress the second commandment there are no paintings or sculptures in the synagogue. Decoration, if any, usually consists of quotations in Hebrew from the Scriptures.

A CHANGING FAITH

The foregoing account reflects in outline and in general terms Jewish practice and custom as it developed almost unchanged from talmudic times. But Jewish thought and practice have constantly been affected by the historical experience of the Jewish people. From the period of the Babylonian exile in the sixth century B.C., the Jews spread far and wide throughout the world. In the time of the Roman Empire they could be found everywhere throughout Europe and the Middle East, and they continued to travel further afield into Asia, Africa and the Americas. It was natural, therefore, that they should adopt to a certain extent the way of life of the peoples among whom they lived, and so we do find differences in practice between a Jewish community in London, shall we say, and another community in Persia. There are significant differences between the *Ashkenazim* (Northern and Eastern European Jews) and *Sefardim* (Mediterranean and Arabic-speaking Jews). But the basic structure of belief and practice remained the same. One of the strengths of the Jewish people has been that wherever he goes a Jew can usually find a community of his own people whose practices he understands and among whom he can feel himself to be a welcome guest.

But there are other features, apart from geographical ones, which have influenced the Jewish character and the Jewish religion. Many of their customs, particularly their dietary laws and other domestic ceremonials, have helped to preserve the distinctive character of the Jewish people. But this distinctiveness has not always been of their own choosing. In many lands and ages the Jews have been considered a people apart, and they have often been persecuted and oppressed. Many reasons have been given for the great suffering that has been inflicted upon the Jewish people, culminating in the death of some six million at the hands of the Nazis and their collaborators during the Second World War. A minority group is often used as a scapegoat for the shortcomings, disappointments and frustrations of the society in which it lives, and no doubt a great deal of anti-semitism in the past can be put down

to this factor. But an important cause of some of the most
virulent anti-Jewish outbreaks, particularly in Europe,
has been the teaching of the Christian Church concerning
the role that the Jews were supposed to have played in
the trial and death of Jesus of Nazareth. The Jew was
regarded as an outcast because the Church taught that
he belonged to a people that had encompassed the death of
'the son of God'. It was a case of what one might call
'inherited guilt'. Most scholars, including Churchmen
(especially after the declaration of Pope John XXIII that
absolved the Jews of 'deicide'), now acknowledge that
there is no historical foundation for the imposition of
guilt upon the Jewish people as a whole for the death of
Jesus. His trial and execution were primarily politically
motivated by the Roman government. In any case, from
the Jewish point of view, Jesus, who was brought up as a
Jew, and who never forsook Judaism, taught to his followers that Judaism which he had learnt from his teachers,
coloured as it was with the messianic expectations that
were current among the Jews at that time. It is only comparatively recently that Jews and Christians have been
able to sit down together and discuss their respective
beliefs on a basis of equality and mutual understanding,
and the previous intense antagonism that the Church
officially displayed towards the Jewish people is now
gradually becoming a thing of the past.

The Jews have always been susceptible to the influence
of other cultures, and this has shown itself particularly in
the developments that have taken place in Jewish thought.
There is no authoritative system of Jewish belief. Judaism
is an undogmatic religion, more concerned, in the traditional form, with correct practice and action, rather than
with doctrine. This has permitted considerable flexibility
in Jewish ideas, and there has been a wide range of different presentations of Judaism, ranging from the mystical
conception, portrayed particularly in the pages of the

84

Zohar from the late thirteenth century, to the extremely rationalistic approach exemplified by the great philosopher Moses Maimonides (1135–1204) and his followers.

It is important to remember that Judaism is not a single monolithic structure. There have always been differences of emphasis among Jewish communities, witness the conflict between the Sadducees and the Pharisees, the Karaites and the Rabbanites, the Hasidim and their opponents. This variety of Jewish belief and practice is particularly evident in our own time. During the Middle Ages when, for the most part, Jews were discriminated against and were not allowed to pursue certain trades and professions, or permitted to study at European universities or other schools of learning, they were a much more closely knit community, following the religious life bequeathed to them by their ancestors. However, after the emancipation in Europe, in the late eighteenth and early nineteenth centuries, Jews were allowed to mix freely in most social circles, could attend centres of higher learning, and follow the more specialised professions. They thus became imbued with nineteenth-century European idealism and this affected their attitude to Judaism. Some of them determined to reform Jewish belief and practice. They adopted a more intellectual approach, abolishing belief in a personal messiah, in physical resurrection, and even in the divine authorship of the *Torah*, which was, and is, a cornerstone of orthodox Judaism, substituting for it a belief in 'progressive revelation'. They placed more emphasis on ethics than on ritual. They realised that many Jews, even if they could read the Hebrew language, could not understand it, and so they began to recite prayers in the language which they normally spoke in the country where they lived. Thus began the Reform and Liberal movements in Judaism which spread rapidly, particularly in the United States.

Jews also became affected by the growing ideas of

nationalism in nineteenth-century Europe. We have already seen that the concept of nationhood was an integral part of the Jewish character, although it was combined with a number of other elements. During the last century, the national aspect came very much to the fore, and a Zionist movement developed which in its extreme form propagated a solely nationalistic view of the Jewish people, and campaigned for a national homeland in the ancient birthplace of the Jewish people in Palestine. This campaign was given a great impetus by the terrible suffering of the Jewish people during the Nazi holocaust, and a refuge for the persecuted was established by the United Nations in the independent State of Israel in 1948. This, however, gave rise to new conflicts which have caused much destruction to the lives and property of countless Jews and Arabs in the Middle East.

The Jews remain comparatively few in number. It is estimated that there are some 13 million in the world today, of whom about six million live in America, two to three million in the Soviet Union, and nearly two million in the State of Israel. The United Kingdom has about 450,000 Jews, of whom the greater part live in London and the home counties. Some of these can trace their English ancestry back to the Jews who were readmitted to this country by Oliver Cromwell in 1656, but most of them are descended from later waves of Jewish immigrants who fled from the pogroms in Eastern Europe in the late nineteenth century, or who found a refuge here in more recent times from the concentration camps of Nazi Germany.

Like most religious minorities, Jews have a constant struggle to retain their distinctive identity and to resist the forces of assimilation. The percentage of marriage with non-Jews in the United Kingdom is quite high, between 15 per cent and 20 per cent of all marriages involving Jews, and this figure may be higher in the United States. There is a likelihood, of course, that the children of such marriages will not be brought up as Jews, with a consequent decline in the numbers of those professing the Jewish faith. In addition, Jews, in common with other religious groups, have to face the challenges that scientific materialism and atheistic philosophies present to religious thought and way of life. Judaism's flexibility in theology, however, is extremely valuable here.

Leaders of Jewry have to strive to ensure that members of their congregations and their children gain an appreciation of the worth of Jewish culture and the continuing validity of the Jewish ethic, which has so influenced the moral principles of Christianity and thereby the whole European outlook on life. The Jews have long cherished their unique religious culture; they have been prepared to suffer in countless numbers for their beliefs, and they will continue to bear witness to the God-given mission that was accorded to them at the very beginning of their history.

FOR FURTHER READING:

B. J. Bamberger: *The Story of Judaism* (Union of American Hebrew Congregations).
J. Browne: *The Wisdom of Israel* (Joseph).
A. Cohen: *Everyman's Talmud* (Dent).
I. Epstein: *Judaism* (Pelican Books).
J. Parkes: *History of the Jewish People* (Pelican Books).
Pearl and Brookes: *A Guide to Jewish Knowledge* (Jewish Chronicle Publications).
L. Roth: *Judaism* (Faber).
Werblowsky and Wigoder: *The Encyclopaedia of the Jewish Religion* (Dent).

FOR INFORMATION:

United Synagogue, Woburn House, Upper Woburn Place, London W.C.1.

Reform Synagogues of Great Britain, 33 Seymour Place,
London W.1.

Union of Liberal and Progressive Synagogues, 109
Whitfield Street, London W.1.

Council of Christians and Jews, 41 Cadogan Gardens,
London S.W.3.

Jewish Information Service, 34 Upper Berkeley Street,
London W1H 7PG.

CHAPTER

6

The Christians

The name 'Christian' was used for the first time in a city
in the Roman empire 1900 years ago. The place was
Antioch in Syria, to the north of Palestine—now part of
the country of Turkey. In the first century it was one of
the three most important cities in the Roman world. It
was a meeting place of east and west and the population
included a great variety of people—Romans, Greeks,
Syrians, Jews, Asians. Many practices and beliefs were
represented among the million or more inhabitants. There
were clubs for various purposes, there were religious
societies which people joined by going through a secret
ceremony in which they achieved union with a god, and
strange cults that practised magic and astrology. In the
streets could be seen temples to the Greek and Roman
gods and synagogues of the Jews. During the years A.D.
40–45 a new society began to attract attention. Some of
the members were Jews, but there were non-Jews amongst
them also; this in itself was strange, for the Jews generally
kept strictly to themselves. These people were speaking
about a man who had lived some dozen years before in
Palestine and had been put to death by the Roman
governor. They declared that he was the Messiah, the
deliverer whom the Jews had for a long time been expect-

ing, who would restore their nation. At Antioch they used the Greek word for this, the deliverer or anointed, Christos. The inhabitants rather prided themselves on their wit and were ready to make fun of people who were in any way peculiar. So someone suggested these queer people should be called Christos-ones or Christians and the term, first given as a nickname, stuck.

We have evidence of the existence of these Christians in other parts of the empire as well. The historian Tacitus tells of the fire of Rome in A.D. 64 and how the emperor Nero, to counter the rumours that he himself had been responsible for the outbreak, suggested that the Christians were to blame. Tacitus goes on to say that this sect (which he calls a 'wretched superstition') had been founded by one Christus, who had been executed by Pontius Pilate in the reign of the emperor Tiberius, and had since spread throughout the empire. Another Roman writer, Suetonius, says that the emperor Claudius expelled Jews from Rome in A.D. 49, because they were causing touble, instigated by 'Chrestus'. This is generally taken to refer to trouble between Jews and Christians. The Roman authorities thought that the ringleader was someone called Chrestus or Christus. Early in the second century Pliny, governor of the province of Bithynia in Asia Minor, wrote to his friend the emperor Trajan asking for advice as to how he should deal with the people called Christians and gave him an account of what he had been able to find out about them and their founder. Jewish writers of the same period also refer to the work, teaching and death of Jesus.

The rise of Christianity is thus firmly placed in history. None of these writers had any doubt that Christ had lived, taught and died in the reign of Tiberius during the governorship of Pontius Pilate, who was procurator of Judea from A.D. 26 to 36. So an investigation into the nature of Christianity must start with some account of Jesus of Nazareth.

By the first century, Palestine—the land now divided between the states of Israel and Jordan—had already had a long and varied history, in the course of which the inhabitants had endured much suffering. They had been under the rule of one foreign power after another—Egyptians, Assyrians, Babylonians, Persians, Greeks, Romans. It was then part of the Roman province of Syria. It was a turbulent land, where people argued violently and acted violently. The Jewish inhabitants were at one in hating their Roman rulers, but were divided on the best way of getting rid of them. Some were for patient endurance, believing that God would deliver them in his own good time if they kept faithful to their religion. Others were for direct action, thinking that it was the purpose of God that the Romans should be driven out by force. Different sects of the Jews also argued about their religion. All Jews were agreed on their basic beliefs—that there was only one God (they were the only people in the Roman world who held this) and that he asked for a high standard of conduct. Religion (a man's attitude towards God) and morality (his attitude towards his fellows) were firmly linked together in Judaism. There was also a widespread expectation among the Jews that one day God would establish his rule over men's lives. A new era would begin—the kingdom, or reign of God. The vital question was: How would this come about? Some held that it would be by forceful political action on the part of the Jews and they were prepared to bring about the kingdom of God by violence. Some looked for a super-natural act of God himself, while yet others trusted that it would come by their quiet and patient observance of the Law and the duties of their religion.

In the midst of this explosive situation, in A.D. 28–29, a strange wild figure emerged from the wilderness of

Judea, a tract of heathland west of the Dead Sea. He denounced the nation for its evil ways, warned the people of a coming judgment and called on them to repent. This man, John, called the baptiser from his demand that the people should wash in the Jordan as a sign of their change of life, stirred the people of Palestine as the prophets of old had done and awoke their eager expectation, for he also spoke of a successor who would be greater than he was. Unfortunately he was unable to continue his work, for the local Jewish ruler had him arrested and imprisoned. Shortly afterwards a carpenter from the town of Nazareth in Galilee, named Joshua (or Jesus) began to preach in the synagogues and to crowds in the open air. His message was that the expected new era had arrived—'the kingdom of God is at hand', he declared. He called upon the Jews to awake to this situation, to change their outlook, their way of life and their thinking. By sayings and parables he described what the rule of God was like and what it would mean in men's lives. He sought to challenge his hearers: God's rule is present and a new way of life is possible; what are you going to do about it?

Jesus also healed people, mostly those who suffered from what today we would call psychosomatic disorders— paralysis, hysteria, epileptic fits, fever, skin diseases. These 'miracles' of healing at least are well vouched for and are considered today to be quite credible. Jesus himself regarded them as evidence of the power of God. When his enemies challenged him by accusing him of 'driving out demons' (the contemporary way of describing many of these cures) by using the power of the devil, he suggested an alternative explanation: 'If I do these things by the Spirit (or agency) of God, then the kingdom of God has arrived among you'.

His words and his deeds caused great excitement throughout Palestine. If he had taken advantage of this, he could have been a great popular hero. But he deliberately avoided publicity, telling people whom he cured to say nothing about it to anyone. At the beginning of his public work he faced and rejected the temptation to adopt the role of a Messiah who would work wonders to attract people to himself, or a deliverer who would exercise force to set up God's reign. The Zealots, religious and political extremists who were incessantly plotting against the Romans, would have supported him if he had taken their way. But Jesus warned the Jews of the consequences of such a course—that it would mean the end of their nation and the destruction of Jerusalem. He told people that they should love their enemies and do good to them instead of retaliating against those who hurt them, that they should treat others as they would wish to be treated themselves, that they should exercise tolerance. That, he said, was the way in which God treated men and they could be true children of God by acting as he did. He insisted that the inner spirit of a man, his thoughts and motives, were more important than the outward observance of rules and regulations. He shocked the strict religious folk by mixing with disreputable people whom they classed as 'sinners'— people who did not observe all the practices of the Jewish religion, tax-collectors who worked for their rulers, women with a bad reputation. He allowed his disciples to break the strict laws of Sabbath observance and of fasting and mere outward ceremonies. The only people whom he denounced were those who were outwardly religious but whose attitude and motives were wrong. He called them 'hypocrites'; they were only playing a part and their religion was a matter of form without deep conviction.

Among the common people of Galilee, the northern part of Palestine where he spent most of his time, Jesus soon became very popular. They wondered at the authority with which he spoke, so different from the usual teachers in the synagogues, and crowds flocked to him in the towns and followed him into the open country. They felt that here was someone who did not express contempt for them as did many of their leaders. He told them that God was a Father who cared for the least of his children. He stirred them to new hope by his proclamation that the kingdom of God was a reality and present among them and was open to all. He refused to lay down hard and fast rules which had to be followed exactly in order to gain acceptance by God. He called the people to join a new family, declaring that those who did the will of God were his brothers and sisters, and to enjoy a spiritual fellowship which transcended barriers of caste and class, race and colour. Although his work was confined mainly to his own people, the Jews, he envisaged a world-wide kingdom of God to which people from all points of the compass would come.

Jesus made no claims for himself. When demented people, with the insight which frequently accompanies abnormal mental states, acclaimed him as 'God's holy one' or 'son of God', he sternly told them to keep silent. When his disciple Peter declared that Jesus was the expected Messiah, his immediate reaction was to command the disciples to tell nobody. The only time he admitted to being the Messiah was at his trial, when the high priest challenged him to say if he was 'the son of the Blessed', and even then his reply was ambiguous. Jesus saw that he could not fit into any accepted messianic category, for his idea of messiahship was far different from that of his contemporaries. His conception of greatness was that of service. He realised that to carry out such an ideal would mean suffering and rejection by his own people. Yet from the authority of his words—'I say to you', he declared when amending the laws of the Old Testament— his demand for personal loyalty and his claim that his work was evidence of the presence of the rule of God, it was clear that here was no ordinary 'simple religious teacher'.

In his own district of Galilee there was opposition to Jesus from the strict orthodox Jews, many of whom belonged to the Pharisee party, mainly on small points of observance of the Jewish law and regulations. He faced real danger, however, when he visited Jerusalem for the Passover festival. There, in the capital city, he came up against the priests of the Jewish religion, whose chief interest was in the maintenance of the temple and its elaborate system of ritual and sacrifices. Jesus was indignant at the trading which was carried on, with their connivance, in the outer Court of the Gentiles which surrounded the whole temple area and he ordered those who were selling animals for sacrifice and changing the Roman money into Jewish coinage to leave the temple. This was a direct challenge to the authority of the priests and rulers, and against them a provincial teacher, with little support in Jerusalem, was powerless. He was eventually arrested and brought to trial before the Sanhedrin, the native Jewish council to which the Romans allowed certain powers. There he was charged with attacking Judaism—'threatening to destroy the temple' was the crude way in which they put it. Anxious to get rid of this idealist, with his talk of another temple—the invisible kingdom of God—which was to replace theirs, and fearing a popular movement in his favour which might endanger their standing with the Romans and their national privileges, the Jewish rulers brought him before the Roman governor Pontius Pilate with the accusation that he was proclaiming himself as king. This was a political matter which any Roman ruler would have dealt with, for nobody was allowed to set himself up as king without the permission of the emperor; and it was on this ground that, by the rough and ready justice meted out by the Romans to subject races, he was executed by crucifixion.

The death of Jesus, on the day we call Good Friday, was not, however, the end. He left a small band of men and

women as his followers, who were at first utterly dis-
pirited at what appeared to be the failure of their master's
cause. It is not quite clear from the account in the Gospels
what they did after the crucifixion, whether they returned
to Galilee on the completion of the Passover days or
whether they remained in Jerusalem until the next festival
called Pentecost, which occurred seven weeks later. The
one thing that the records are agreed on is that they
became convinced that the death of Jesus had not been a
tragedy but a triumph, that he was alive and they were to
carry on the work which he had begun. The experiences
of the disciples are recounted as a series of appearances of
Jesus. The earliest list of these occurs in a letter which Paul
wrote about twenty-five years after the crucifixion. He
says that Jesus was first seen by Peter, then by a large
number of others apart from the apostles, by James, one
of Jesus' own brothers, and last of all by Paul himself,
about four years later. There is also in the Gospels a story
about some women who visited the tomb where Jesus'
body had been put, but it was not there. What the disciples
emphasised was that Jesus was not a dead teacher but a
living master. Now full of boldness, they proclaimed, first
at Jerusalem and then further afield, that Jesus was the
Messiah, that he had inaugurated a new era, the messianic age. They claimed that men could be brought into
a new relationship with God which would change their
whole outlook and save them from their weaknesses and
sins. They declared that men could obtain this new
experience of life through belief in Jesus and by adopting
an attitude of trust and loyalty which they called 'faith'.
Those who accepted their message were enrolled in the
society of disciples which they called the 'church'. The
Greek word *ekklēsia* was the one used for the meeting of
the citizens summoned to deal with the affairs of the
ancient city-states of Greece. It was also the term for the
assembly of the Hebrew tribes in Old Testament times

and the disciples of Jesus considered that they constituted a 'new Israel'.

THE DEVELOPMENT OF THE CHURCH

At first the work of the church was confined to the Jews, but on the whole they rejected the message. Gradually realisation came that the message about Jesus must be passed on to all, although this decision was not made without much discussion and a controversy which nearly split the early church. So Christianity became a Gentile movement. Missionaries such as Paul turned towards Europe. Before the end of the first century groups of Christians were to be found in almost every city of the Roman empire. For two hundred years they suffered persecution, but the attempts of emperors and provincial governors to stamp out the church proved futile and it grew rapidly. Eventually the emperor Constantine realised that it was impossible to suppress it and in the year A.D. 313 Christianity was recognised as one of the 'permitted' religions of the empire. Within a few centuries it became the official religion of Europe. Missionaries went out in all directions, to north and south America, the West Indies, Africa, India, China. Today Christianity is one of the great world religions, with adherents in every country and continent.

This expansion was accompanied by a development in ideas and the way in which Christians expressed their beliefs. To the earliest Jewish disciples Jesus was the Messiah, the anointed one of God. They also called him Son of God. This term originally meant a man who reflected in his life the character of God himself; Jesus said that the peacemakers and those who forgave their enemies were sons of God. It became a title for the Jewish Messiah, sent by God to establish his kingdom. In the first century the term was also used in some places to denote a supernatural being who had existed in heaven before he came to live among men on earth and in this sense it was applied to Jesus by preachers such as Paul. Jesus was also called the Wisdom of God—a title borrowed from the Jews, who had personified this divine attribute. The Christians also adopted a term which was common to both Jewish and Greek thought—the Word (*Logos*). This was conceived as a means by which God communicated with men. Towards the end of the first century an account of the life of Jesus was produced which was dominated by this thought and the deeds and teaching of Jesus were portrayed as the manifestation of the divine *Logos* among men.

The Christians also claimed that they had an experience of the Spirit of God. In the Hebrew scriptures God was frequently spoken of as Spirit and it was by his Spirit that he spoke with men like the prophets and acted through them. Jesus had told his followers that God's Spirit would guide them and support them in their trials. The Christians also knew God as Father. So gradually there developed through the first four centuries a doctrine of a 'Trinity', that there were three aspects of the activity of God, that he could be known as Father, that he could be approached through Jesus and that he could be inwardly experienced as Spirit.

Arguments also developed in the church which led to disputes, sometimes conducted with bitter feeling and words, about the nature of Christian beliefs and the way in which these should be expressed. The outcome of these controversies was the formation of statements which are known as the 'historic creeds', which were drawn up by various church councils in the fourth and fifth centuries.

THREE CHRISTIAN PRINCIPLES

During the centuries which have passed since those early

years many changes have come about in the church and it may seem that Christians of today have little in common with the first disciples of Jesus. But there are certain basic principles which may be regarded as essential for Christian people of every age:

(i) *Belief in God.* Christianity, Judaism and Islam are the three great monotheistic religions. God may be found by men in many ways. Some find him in history, some in nature, some in music and art, some in human life and experience at its highest or deepest; the Christian emphasis is that above all he is shown in the life and teaching of Jesus. So God to the Christian is not primarily creator or judge, but Father. Any idea of God which is inconsistent with the character of Jesus himself is ruled out.

To say 'I believe in God' is not a mere verbal assent to a statement in a creed or an assertion of the 'existence' of God. It is rather a conviction that God matters and must be taken into account in any view of the meaning of the world and of human life. It is an assertion that the ultimate reality in the universe, the source of our being and the ground of our relations with other people, is personal. We have to use this term because the highest ideas and ideals which we know are those of persons, although we realise that this and any other terms used about ultimate reality are bound to be inadequate. The least inadequate name for God is the one which Jesus used to express the relationship between God and men—Father.

(ii) *Allegiance to Christ.* The earliest Christian creed consisted of three words—'Jesus is lord'. The Christians put him at the centre of their lives and the test of any thought or action which they contemplated was: Would this be in accordance with the teaching and spirit of Jesus? When he was on earth Jesus' words to those who would be his disciples were simply: 'Follow me'. To carry out this fundamental demand has often meant different things to different people and Christians have tried to express their loyalty to Jesus in many various ways. Churches through-out the world—or rather sections of the universal Christian church—have emphasised different aspects of this. Con-sidering that the church includes people of many races and cultures and national traditions, it is inevitable that there should be varieties of ecclesiastical organisation and modes of worship, that there should be differences in their ways of expressing their beliefs, that some should emphasise one aspect of the teaching of Jesus or one phase of Christian practice and some another. But for all Christians alle-giance to Jesus should mean a rethinking of their lives, beliefs and actions in the light of the demands of Jesus himself.

(*iii*) '*Christian action*' in its widest sense is an essential part of the life of people for whom Christ is central. Jesus himself endorsed two commandments or ideals from the Old Testament—to love God with all one's might and mind and to love one's neighbour as oneself. The early Christians expressed their attitude towards their fellow men by using a Greek word (*agapē*) which is generally translated 'love' (an older rendering was 'charity'). It really means caring, showing consideration for others, even at the expense of one's own comfort, welfare or even life. That is why there have been in all ages Christians who have given themselves to education, to social and medical work, to feeding the hungry, to helping people who have been stricken by natural disasters or who have been suffering as a result of war or the cruelty of men.

The Christian sees a world which is in dire need of change, where many things are incompatible with the spirit of Christ. So he is opposed to such evils as slavery, war, exploitation, cruelty, oppression, ignorance and the denial of human rights and liberties to people on grounds of social class or caste or colour or race. Many consider that it is the task of Christians not merely to protest at such things and to alleviate the sufferings of the poor, the dispossessed, the outcast and the oppressed, but to change a system which can produce such a state of affairs. The efforts of Christian people have often been misunderstood and misinterpreted but their activities in the political, social, educational and international fields spring from their loyalty to Christ and the attitude of Jesus himself. He saw something of God in every man; although he realised the frailties of human nature, he respected people and believed in their possibilities. So the motive which impels his followers to such activities is the realisation of the value of the individual as a child of God and their response to the demand of Jesus.

The three Christian essentials—the conviction of God, as Father, allegiance to the spirit of Christ and practical action—thus all spring from the fundamental command, 'Follow me'. Wherever they are followed, they are proof that Christianity is still a living force in the world.

Note. It may be considered by some readers that this chapter gives an inadequate account of 'The Christians', compared with the detailed statements of the beliefs and practices of the religions which are described in the other parts of this book. Little is said here about theological beliefs, nothing about the various forms of worship in the different Christian traditions; there is no mention of sacramental views and observances, no account of the 'denominations' which are a feature of the Christian community in many countries and no consideration of the function of the church and the nature of the ministry which are frequently subjects of debate in proposals for union between different churches.

Such matters have been deliberately omitted here, for a specific reason. The other religious systems treated in this book will be comparatively unknown to most readers. The writers have had to explain forms of belief and practices which in some ways may seem alien to our thought and way of life. For many this will be the only way in which they can gain acquaintance with the principles held by Hindus, Buddhists, Confucianists, Shintoists, Jews, Sikhs or Muslims. Knowledge about Christianity, on the other hand, is readily available to anyone who will take a small amount of trouble to find out. In village, town and city there are people to whom an enquirer can go for information or advice—the rector or vicar of the parish, a Free Church minister, a priest of the Roman Catholic church or at least an informed layman. In addition, within easy reach of almost every home in the land there is a building of some kind where one can join in Christian worship. There are also in every bookshop numerous books which deal with various aspects of Christian thought and practice, many of them quite inexpensive. In view of this wealth of material which is available, only the funda- mental matters in which all branches of the church share have been covered—the historical origin of Christianity and the principles which may be said to constitute the essentials for anything that can truly be called 'Christian'.

FOR FURTHER READING:

S. C. Carpenter: *Christianity* (Pelican Books).
F. W. Dillistone: *The Christian Faith* (Hodder and Stoughton).
C. H. Dodd: *The Founder of Christianity* (Collins).
E. A. Payne: *The Growth of the World Church* (Macmillan).
K. Slack: *The British Churches Today* (S.C.M.).
J. W. C. Wand: *History of the Modern Church* (Methuen).

FOR INFORMATION:

British Council of Churches, 10 Eaton Gate, Sloane Square, London S.W.1.

Catholic Truth Society, 40 Eccleston Square, London S.W.1.

Church of England Information Office, Church House, Dean's Yard, London S.W.1.

Free Church Federal Council, 27 Tavistock Square, London W.C.1.

7

The Muslims

Man's actions are generally governed by his thinking and one cannot understand a person's behaviour unless one tries to understand his way of thinking. To understand Muslims and Islam it is therefore necessary to know what makes them Muslims, as they are a people whose identity is based on certain ideas and not on any belief in race, nationality or colour.

ISLAM

Popular beliefs like old wives' tales can often be far removed from the truth. To many people Islam is a religion that was started by Mohammad and the people who followed him are called Mohammadens. This, however, is quite different from what Muslims think about Islam and themselves. The word Islam has two meanings: (a) Submission, that is to submit to the guidance of God and live according to his advice. (b) Peace, that is to live with peace within one's self and peace around one's self. Islam is therefore an attitude of life, an attitude that consists of submission to God. This attitude, it claims, will result in peace of mind, which it regards as a prerequisite for the proper functioning of life.

According to Islamic belief, man and whatever surrounds him, such as this earth that he lives upon, the laws of nature that are operating in different ways and in different fields, the stars and the oceans, were all created by God who has therefore exact knowledge of their nature and their working. He is a Being who is all-knowing and, therefore, the best qualified to give guidance on any subject that concerns man and his different needs and functions. Muslims believe that all suffering, whether personal or national, is the result of wrong thinking and wrong actions, and can be removed if man accepts the right guidance and acts in accordance with such advice. Man will then be able to live in peace and progress in happiness.

Such guidance can come only from God—the maker and knower of all things—and so to live by his advice is the only way to live in peace and happiness. That is what Islam is about. God, being the creator of man, has naturally a responsibility towards him, namely to guide him according to his knowledge of various things and, as God is one and human beings are the same in spite of differences of colour, features or period of time, his guidance must also be the same for all his people of all times and places.

In any human problem, man is the most important factor to be considered. Thus people who commit big robberies are not poor people who are in desperate need of money, and conversely people who help others may not necessarily be rich. One may be dishonest in spite of being in a good position and one may be truthful although one may be in difficult circumstances. A person's actions are dependent on the way in which he thinks and God has always endeavoured to correct his thinking. It is also true that to a human being the example and experience of another person like himself are more true and profitable than the example of someone with whom he does not share problems or needs. The religion of Islam, therefore, maintains that God has always sent his guidance to mankind in all ages of history through members of the human race whom he chose, because of their qualities of mind and character, for the truthful conveyance of his message, as well as to be an example to their fellow men and women. Such persons are called in Islam the messengers of God, men who were remarkably outstanding personalities of their times. Their enquiry led them to a belief in God and they were selected by God on their merits for the office of conveying his message to mankind. Adam, as the first human being that lived on this earth, was the first person to whom this guidance was given. Since then there have been many messengers of God—Abraham, Noah, Isaac, Ishmael, Moses, Jesus, to name but a few—who conveyed the same divine message to their fellow men, to keep them on the right path and save them from all harm. The advice they brought was compiled and is referred to as the Book of God. We may call the books by different names, such as the Torah or Bible, but they all contain basically the same divine message.

At this period of history which may be said to mark the beginning of the modern age, Mohammad, the last messenger of God, was chosen and commanded to convey the divine message to the human race. The advice he brought is compiled in the book we know as the Qur-aan (Quran or Koran). It was about A.D. 610 that Mohammad, who was born in A.D. 570, began to convey the divine message, and the concepts and commands that form the present-day Islam were revealed to him over a period of twenty-three years.

THE SITUATION AT THE TIME OF MOHAMMAD

In our modern way of speaking, one may say that the world of the sixth century A.D. was dominated by two powerful blocs, namely the Persian and the Roman empires, who were intermittently at war with each other. There were also a number of uncommitted and backward nations that were under the influence of one or the other of the main powers or were the victims of both. The Roman and the Persian empires both represented what had once been great civilisations but, as is always the case when civilisations begin to decay, their culture was marked by hypocrisy, untruthfulness, injustice, exploitation and insecurity, and the love of ease, money and pleasure. Under the cover of 'civilisation' and the pretensions of culture, each man's first thought was for himself and he was much less concerned for his fellow men. The society, though civilised in name, was not much different in essence from other so-called 'uncivilised' societies and nations, as greed and lack of care for one's fellow men were the order of the day and, because there was no firm belief in moral values like truth, honesty, faithfulness, right and wrong, people felt insecure and frustrated. There were wars involving the major powers and consequently much human suffering for causes that in truth and fairness could not be justified. The victorious nations took their defeated enemies, including the women and children, as their slaves and treated them as chattels who had no rights or privileges.

The people of the 'uncivilised' nations, of which Arabia was a typical example, had many basic good qualities of character like courage, a pride in the ability to do hard work, hospitality, frankness, simplicity, but they were so ignorant that they could hardly turn these qualities to any advantage to themselves. They were organised on the basis of tribes and families instead of in cities and towns, and pride and prejudice caused innumerable conflicts and much killing among their people. They worshipped idols whose wishes were interpreted by priests according to their discretion and disposition and the rest of the people were obliged to follow their direction. Many of the tribes preferred to live a nomadic life and the plundering of other people was a way of earning their livelihood. Women had not much status or respect in their society and to many it seemed a shame to have a daughter, and it was not unusual for a father to bury his daughter alive to keep his honour safe.

There was no central government as in the neighbouring Roman and Persian empires and, as the nomadic tribes felt free to live on plunder, these two empires also felt free to attack their ignorant neighbours and enjoy their loot.

THE LIFE OF MOHAMMAD

This was the state of affairs when Mohammad began to preach that there was one God who had created us all and all that surrounds us, to whom we will return one day to give an account of what we do in this worldly life. Life was a great opportunity, qualities were the gift of God, all men and women were the creation of God and so were brothers and sisters to each other and equal in law. There are fundamental rights determined by the wisdom of God which we all must uphold and there are fundamental wrongs declared such by God which we all must condemn and from which we should refrain. This preaching, although it appealed to the young and the poor in his society and those who were intellectually honest and unbiased, angered those who felt that acceptance of his message would mean good-bye to their bad practices, as well as their social position and authority. They became his bitter enemies and planned to do all that they could to stop him from carrying on his mission. He was personally insulted at every gathering where he stood to address people, stones were thrown at him, thorns were spread in his way and rubbish was thrown on his head.

The enemies of Mohammad did not stop with personal

persecution, but turned their wrath against his followers as well. The weak and poor among them were the worse hit and were subjected to all imaginable tortures. They were beaten with sticks, pulled on the hot sand and made to lie there with heavy stones on their chests. Some lost their lives. When their sufferings became unbearable, some of Mohammad's followers decided to emigrate to Abyssinia. This occurred about the year A.D. 615 and is called the first Emigration or Hijrah and is an important landmark in the history of the Islamic movement. The Christian king of Abyssinia was a very pious person and after listening to their account of the teaching of Mohammad felt that this was the same as that preached by Jesus Christ in his time. He gave them permission to live in peace in his kingdom.

In Arabia Mohammad was subjected to further persecution. He and his family were expelled from Mecca and forced to live in a barren valley, while his enemies maintained a blockade of all food supplies. They lived thus for three years and ultimately were forced to live on leaves as there was nothing else to eat. After three years some people in Mecca began to feel a sense of shame and revolt at this inhuman treatment of Mohammad and his kinsmen and gathered enough public opinion to lift the blockade of food and let them return to the city. Mohammad started his preaching again and spread his activities to those visitors from other cities who came to Mecca on their annual pilgrimage or for any other reason. He found a good response from delegates who came from Medina, a town about 250 miles north of Mecca. His enemies became furious at his success and decided on a plan to kill him while he was asleep. Mohammad somehow got knowledge of this plan and decided to emigrate to Medina, where a good many people had already accepted Islam and were willing to help him. On the night of the planned murder he managed to escape to Medina. This happened in A.D.

622 and is called the second Emigration or Hijrah. It is of special significance because it forms the first date of the Muslim calendar.

After reaching Medina, Mohammad devoted his attention to the moral and educational uplift of his people and began to organise his society into a Muslim state. People were taught to live and progress according to the teachings of the Quran and his government was run on the same principles. The people of Mecca became more jealous and angry at his success and with the help of other tribes and towns tried to invade Medina, but were defeated on all occasions. Still the enemies of his message did not allow peace to his followers; they were attacked at every opportunity and peace terms and promises were broken at will. At last Mohammad got tired of this situation and decided to invade Mecca and bring an end to this continual disturbance. This he did in A.D. 630. His enemies were taken by surprise and the city fell without any bloodshed. Thereafter Mohammad spent the rest of his life conveying the divine guidance to his people in peace and made efforts to extend the same to the neighbouring countries. He died in A.D. 632.

BELIEFS IN ISLAM

The teaching of Islam is very simple and the various practices that a Muslim is required to observe are but a means to make these teachings become a living force in the daily life of a Muslim. The doctrines of Islam are: (*i*) belief in a God, who is the all-pervading, ever-existing Reality; (*ii*) belief in the messengers of God, who brought and preached the way of life recommended by the Creator of mankind; (*iii*) belief in the books of God; (*iv*) belief in angels, whose nature we do not know but who we are given to understand are entities that are entrusted by God to do certain tasks. They have no will of their own but carry out the commands with implicit obedience; (v) belief in the day of judgment and life after death.

The most important thought in Islam is that of man's accountability to God who created him for a higher purpose and to whom everyone will be answerable on the day of judgment. Muslims believe that one day this order of things or phase of life will come to an end. The life of this world is considered to be a temporary life, a proving ground or a maturing phase, whereas the permanent life will be in the hereafter. The circumstances of existence in the life after death are dependent on the actions and deeds of this life, which is an opportunity for betterment and evolution, and the perfecting of one's character. To have a good everlasting life in the hereafter a person is required to do good deeds in this life and, conversely, to avoid a long suffering in life after death a person is required to abstain from bad deeds in this life. One must always be just and kind, promises must be fulfilled and obligations must be discharged.

All human beings are the creation of God and therefore equal in law. The basis of respect for others is not money, colour or race, but character. Human life is sacred and must not be taken away except through a due process of law. Theft, cheating and killing are unlawful, lying is forbidden, the relation between the sexes is sacred and must be contracted with due legal form. Every human being has a duty to family, relations, neighbours and society. Slander, jealousy and back-biting are hateful in the eyes of God. Fellow-feeling, self-sacrifice and consideration for others are commendable in the divine view. Man's faculties, abilities, acquisitions and power are responsibilities for the proper discharge of which one is accountable to God.

Man was created by God for some reason, not known to us, but which must be a part of the wider scheme of things of which we have no knowledge. Man was given life and the ability to acquire knowledge and was entrusted with the responsibility of this earth. Life, in the Islamic view, is therefore an office and a responsibility, held by men and women alike. It is not something that we can treat as we please, but something for which we are responsible and have to give an account to the One who gave us that office. All human effort, pursuit and engagement should therefore be approached and shaped in the consciousness of this position and responsibility of man.

The responsibility laid upon man by this concept of him as God's vicegerent on earth is twofold: (a) to develop his personality to its maximum potential; (b) to develop and organise this earth to its maximum potential and in the best manner. This is therefore the task set for man by Islam and the best way to accomplish this task is to lead one's life in obedience to the commands of God. Having the pleasure of God as the motivating force gives the individual a selflessness which makes it possible for him to attain the highest moral standard. As to the objective of the moral code, the Quran briefly describes it as the pursuit of all that is generally and universally good and the avoidance of all that is universally accepted as bad.

RELIGIOUS PRACTICES IN ISLAM

The proper observance of the teachings of Islam is dependent largely on the mental make-up and the character of an individual, and the practices which Muslims observe are the means to build up such a character and mental attitude. These practices are as follows:

Prayer

A Muslim is required to say his prayers five times a day, namely early morning, early afternoon, late afternoon, early evening and late evening. Muslim males are required to observe prayer collectively in their different localities, but the women are allowed to practise at home. On Fridays both males and females are advised to say congregational prayers in the early afternoon in larger gatherings, such as area mosques. The aim of prayer is to inculcate remembrance of God and to remind oneself of being in the presence of God at all times of one's daily life. It is thus hoped that the consciousness of the presence of God and accountability to him will become the dominant mental state of a Muslim and will help him or her to behave correctly in all situations of life.

Fasting

For one month in a lunar year Muslims are required to observe fasting, which means abstaining from drinking, eating and sexual relations from dawn to sunset. This is called the month of Ramadhan. People normally have a meal before dawn and then a meal after sunset. In general this month is regarded as a special period for developing virtues and discarding shortcomings, and so a Muslim is expected to live an exemplary life during this period. The festival of Eid marks the end of Ramadhan and the community celebrates it by offering congregational prayers in large numbers. Both men and women attend these prayers but keep their ranks separate. This is then followed by celebrations and feasting, denoting a sense of satisfaction for having been able to avail oneself of this opportunity of advancing in a spiritual and moral way.

Zakat

A Muslim is required to spend $2\frac{1}{2}$ per cent of his or her annual savings on the needy and the poor. This money is called Zakat, which means that which purifies a person's income. If there is no social or government agency to collect this from people and to spend it on a collective basis, then the individuals have to do it themselves and spend it on people who from their personal knowledge they think are deserving. In principle this represents the religious belief that all people are one family and the needs of the less fortunate are the obligation of those who are in better circumstances.

Hajj

Every Muslim who can afford it is required to make pilgrimage (Hajj) to the House of Kaaba at Mecca, once in his or her own lifetime. It is the House of Kaaba towards which Muslims face while saying their prayers. The culmination of the pilgrimage is marked by an assembly of all pilgrims in the plain of Arafat in Arabia, where they are addressed by their leaders and all matters, religious, political or social, concerning human beings are dicussed. (All congregational prayer meetings, whether on Fridays or Eid, are also used for discussing matters of social importance and the assembly is addressed by a leader chosen by the people.) After the pilgrimage there comes the festival of second Eid, which the pilgrims celebrate by slaughtering animals and feasting each other. The Muslims all over the world do the same as a mark of allegiance to the common cause and celebrate it by organising large congregational prayer, slaughtering animals and meeting and feasting relatives and friends. In principle the practice conveys the concept of the universal brotherhood of man and the sovereignty of God, as people of different nationalities are called together and move towards the symbolic house of God and think of ways of serving him, which in practical terms means serving their fellow beings.

SOCIAL PRACTICES OF MUSLIMS

Marriage

A Muslim marriage is very simple. It only needs two witnesses, before whom the man and the woman agree to accept each other. It is customary on such occasions for a person with good knowledge of the Quran to read out a passage from the Book which reminds them of their duties and obligations to each other. The married couple are then required to take measures to let it be known to other people and this is normally done by inviting relatives and friends to a dinner or a luncheon. The right of divorce is open to either party and is to be exercised only after all possible means to preserve the marriage have failed. Divorce, like marriage, must also be announced to the general public. Muslim males may marry women of other faiths provided they believe in God and the revealed religion and the men may if they so need take more than one wife. Muslim women may marry only Muslims and have one husband.

Food

Muslims may eat all food except pork, birds, or animals, of prey. In slaughtering animals, Muslims are required to do it in such as way that all blood is drained from the body. This is called Halal and is similar to Kosher among the Jews. So Muslims eat either Halal or Kosher meat and abstain from eating other meat. Muslims are forbidden alcohol and are required to avoid all intoxicating products.

Dress

Modesty is the governing principle of Muslim dress design. Nudity and exposure are forbidden and beauty and elegance are required to be sought in covering the human body, while keeping in mind the working conditions and daily needs of people. A dress or design that may cause sexual provocation needs to be avoided.

OTHER ASPECTS OF A MUSLIM'S FAITH

Muslims do not believe that religion should be separate

from the worldly problems of people. They believe that one's spiritual life and one's worldly life are parts of the same individual and cannot be separated from each other. For example, they do not think it is possible for a person to be truthful in spiritual matters and untruthful in politics and still live in mental peace. So they believe in applying religion to every aspect of man's life; this view is responsible for their attitude towards politics, economics and sociology.

Politics

Muslims believe that moral principles of truth, justice, righteousness are sacred and must not be violated for any reason, and that promises must always be kept. Political parties and leaders are expected to work in a spirit of God-consciousness and accountability to him who can never be deceived. There is no wrong that may be justified for the sake of a party, nation, class or country. In principle, rule belongs to God alone, and parliaments, cabinets and leaders who happen to govern other people do so in his name and must bear his spirit and teachings in mind and they can be challenged before a court if they do not do so.

Economics

All the resources of wealth, property, position and office are considered to be a responsibility, for the proper discharge of which a man will be answerable to his Creator; so a man must not consider himself absolutely free to do whatever he likes with his money or his resources. All rights of ownership are with God. People exercise these rights under delegation from him and are therefore required to do so according to his guidance. The right to enjoy and benefit from what God has created is open to all, according to one's ability. Islam does not believe in the absolute equality of all men, but accepts differences of nature, ability and aptitude. It does not believe in equal distribution but in equitable distribution and equal opportunities. Islam accepts the right of ownership but its laws are so designed as to prevent any accumulation of economic powers in one person. Whereas Islam upholds the right of the individual to take from life according to his ability, it is against hoarding the wealth so acquired and keeping it away from circulation. It is the duty of every person to make the best use of all the resources that come into his possession. Hard and conscientious work is encouraged, but Islam prohibits all those means of earning one's livelihood that can result in moral or spiritual loss to society in one way or another. Thus it prohibits gambling and other games of chance and the wastage of time, money and materials. It prohibits all business in which the gain of one party is certain while the gain of the other is uncertain. The right of ownership does not give one the right to waste one's resources. It does not consider that the interests of the employer are by nature opposed to those of the employee, but it holds both to observe justice in dealing with each other, bearing in mind that a Being who is all-knowing knows what is hidden in the minds of men.

Sociology

All men and women, being creations of God, are equal, irrespective of their religion, nationality or colour. They have every right to equal opportunities for improving themselves in life. Therefore Islam does not accept any division of humanity on the basis of colour, race or nationality. On the other hand, it accepts a division which is based on different ideas and concedes the right of all such groups of people to organise their affairs according to their beliefs. It declares that all those who accept Islam belong henceforth to one party, irrespective of their colour or creed, and gives them all equal rights.

To help his fellow human beings is a duty of every

Muslim. Any action or expression that is liable to harm any other person unjustly is forbidden. Islam lays great stress on the sanctity of the family and prohibits all those practices which can be inimical to its interests. Thus fornication and adultery are punishable crimes; marriage is encouraged and celibacy is discouraged. The family is organised on a definite pattern, with the rights and obligations of each member clearly specified. Islam does not accept a loose family system where each is left to act according to his or her own will or desires. It regards the man as the head of the family and all are expected to give him the regard to which his position entitles him. He is not, however, left as an absolute monarch, for his rights are conditioned by the obligations that he owes to his family. Children are required to be obedient and respectful to their parents. A Muslim's concept of the family goes beyond the immediate concern for his wife and children. Relatives and neighbours also have a special significance in his thinking and he feels obliged to care for them.

CONCLUSION

Islam has only one message or invitation that it extends to all mankind—to submit itself to the will of God, the creator and cherisher of all that exists. The type of submission it envisages is total. It does not divide life into the secular and the religious, but accepts and treats it as a unity. Acceptance of Islam therefore means submitting one's life to the will of God in all spheres and aspects of life.

FOR FURTHER READING:

A. N. Dawood: *The Koran* (Penguin Classics).
A. Guillaume: *Islam* (Pelican Books).
S. F. Mahmud: *The Story of Islam* (Oxford).

J. M. Rodwell: *The Koran* (Everyman Paperback—Dent).

W. M. Watts: *Muhammad, Prophet and Statesman* (Oxford).

Obtainable from the Islamic Book Centre, 148 Liverpool
Road, London N.1:

Marmaduke Pickthall: *Quraanic Advices.*
Waheed-ud-Din: *Treasure* (sayings of Muhammad).
Abul-Ala-Maudoodi: *Towards understanding Islam.*
M. Rafi-ud-Din: *The Manifesto of Islam.*
Sayyid Qutb: *The Religion of Islam.*
Shamim Raza: *Introducing the Prophets.*
A. Rahim: *A Short History of Islam.*

FOR INFORMATION:

The Islamic Cultural Book Centre, 148 Liverpool Road,
London N.1.

8

The Sikhs

Among the many Commonwealth citizens who have made their home in Britain and other countries since the early 1950s, there are a large number of Asian origin. They do not all have the same religion and they do not all share the same customs. Those from Pakistan are mainly Muslims, but those from India include the Gujaratis, who are generally Hindus, while those from the Punjab are mainly Sikhs, although some may be Hindus or Muslims. Some of these Asians may have previously emigrated to East Africa, South Africa, Fiji, Guyana or Malaysia and from there they have now come to live amongst us.

The people who come from the Punjab are hardy and ambitious. They want to earn a better living, to give their children a good education and to have better houses and prospects. When India became independent in 1947, the state of Pakistan was created, and the Punjab was divided between the two countries. Muslims remained in the Pakistan part of the Punjab, while the Sikhs and the Hindus went to the Indian part. Nearly all, however, whether Indian or Pakistani, speak Punjabi, while many of them also speak Urdu and Hindi.

A considerable proportion of the Indians who have emigrated are Sikhs and many of these come from a particular district of the Punjab around the city of Jullundur. The Sikhs are mainly distinguishable by their turbans and beards but some of them, especially in the large industrial towns of Britain, have discarded the turban, cut their hair and shaved off their beards. Often, however, they still wear a steel bangle on the right wrist. The women generally wear a cotton dress with a chiffon or net stole thrown over the shoulders and a pair of trousers under the dress. This suit is known as a *salvar-kamiz* (*salvar* being the trousers and *kamiz* the dress). This is the costume of Punjabi women, regardless of their religion, but the Sikh women also wear the steel bangle.

Before the British rule, the Punjab was an independent Sikh state. After its annexation with the rest of India, the Sikhs became known for their large contribution of recruits to the Indian army. They were brave, smart, well-disciplined and loyal. The British army officers learned to have great respect for them. In the Indian Civil Service, too, many Sikhs achieved high positions, but their real qualities and their religious origins remained unknown to the majority of English people, even though books were available on the subject (an Englishman, Max Arthur Macauliffe, published his book, *The Sikh Religion*, in 1909).

The image of the Sikh people primarily as a military sect, was, however, a long way from the truth. The Sikh religion is firmly based on a message of peace and universal brotherhood, and during the 500 years of Sikh history there have been many episodes of courageous, non-violent action in the face of great injustice and brutal oppression. The Sikhs are characteristically brave, tenacious, industrious, generous and hospitable—qualities which are closely connected with the philosophy of life inculcated by their religion.

The Sikh religion dates its origin from Guru Nanak (1469–1539) who was born the son of Hindu parents in the village of Talwandi, now renamed Nankana, in Pakistan not far from Lahore. Kalu, his father, was an accountant and the family were fairly prosperous. Nanak spent much time during his early years in learning about the many different religious sects and their practices, both Hindu and Moslem. He soon became filled with a great love for God and mankind and with contempt for the unnecessary formalities and ceremonies of religious custom. He refused to be invested with the sacred thread as a high caste Hindu and he told the Brahmin priest that the sacred thread worn over the shoulder was powerless to influence a person's behaviour for good or evil. To live a morally good life, to do good actions and to remember God's name, was more important than performing ceremonies, sacrifices and religious pilgrimages.

Nanak refused to worship God through the use of images. He believed that God could be discovered everywhere in creation, within man's own heart, as well as above and beyond the bounds of man's knowledge. Any sincere person, however poor or uneducated, may reach God directly, without the aid of an intermediary, provided that he seeks Him with humble and faithful devotion. God is not born on earth in either human or animal form as a divine incarnation (*avatar*), as the Hindus believed, but He is already present everywhere. Man may reach Him and arrive at a state of complete joy and perfect enlightenment, through following the guidance of a guru (teacher) and by trying to live a life of good actions and by receiving God's grace. Nanak maintained that for man to reach this state, there was no need to retire from the world, to practise severe asceticism, or yoga, or to be celibate. A person may live a perfectly ordinary, working life in his own home, and still remember the name of God and spend some time in meditation, prayer and worship. A good Sikh must never beg or live off the earnings of others, but he must earn his own living honestly, by his own efforts.

Guru Nanak also taught that people must pay for their evil or wrongful actions. If they behave selfishly or cruelly and disregard the needs and rights of others, they will reap for themselves much misery and suffering. This does not come about as a punishment in any hell in the next world, but it is a retribution in this world, perhaps in another birth on earth. Man's soul is an immortal spark of divine light from God himself, and the aim of life should be for the divine spark to merge again into the source of light. Human life and form, with its extra advantages of higher intelligence, speech, free will and manual skill, affords the soul an opportunity to work its way out of ignorance towards that great light which is God himself. Thus, the soul is reborn in human form many times until eventually it reaches such a state of grace that it may become blended again with God.

> As from one fire, millions of sparks arise,
> And though rising separately, unite again in the fire;
> As from one heap of dust, many grains of dust fill
>   the air,
> And filling it, blend with the dust again;
> As in one stream, millions of waves rise up,
> And being water, sink into water again;
> So from God's form emerge
> Non-sentient and sentient beings,
> Who, since they arise from Him,
> Shall merge into Him again.
>   Guru Gobind Singh (*Akal Ustat*, 87)

The spirit of God pervades the whole of His creation, and there is no separation of the material and spiritual elements. It is the intuitive knowledge of this great One-ness of being which is evident in the lives and personalities of the saints or the true Gurus. The Guru is a teacher who gives his whole life to guiding others towards the attainment of this spiritual knowledge, and this he does, not only by his words, but also by his personal example, in his way of life and in his love for mankind. Guru Nanak expressed his belief in the One-ness of God in a verse which is now placed at the beginning of the Sikh holy book:

> There is One God;
> His name is Truth;
> The All-pervading Creator,
> Without fear, without hatred,
> Immortal, Unborn, Self-existent;
> By Grace, the Enlightener.
> True in the beginning, True throughout the ages,
> True even now, Nanak, and forever shall be true.

THE TEN GURUS

While Nanak was still quite young, his parents arranged his marriage to Sulakhni, and in course of time they had two sons. For a while, Nanak worked at Sultanpur as a storekeeper, and there he was joined by the minstrel Mardana, who became his life-long companion. Nanak composed many hymns which Mardana accompanied on the rebeck, and soon he received the divine call to travel abroad and teach his religion to others. He observed that neither the Hindus nor the Moslems truly practised the moral precepts of their religions. They attached more importance to forms and ceremonies than to worshipping God or to living righteously. They were extremely superstitious and allowed their lives to be governed by astrologers, the Brahmin priests and by meaningless rituals.

The Guru's missionary journeys took him all over the Punjab, south to Ceylon, north to the Himalayas, westwards to Mecca, Medina and Baghdad, and eastwards to

Burmah, over a period of forty years, always travelling on foot. He settled at Kartarpur in the Punjab towards the end of his life and it was there that he died after appointing as his successor, Lehna, his most devoted follower, who became known as Guru Angad.

Under the inspiration of Guru Angad, the Sikh religion continued to grow. A free kitchen, called *langar*, was established at Kartarpur, and there everyone was given food together, regardless of their caste, class, race or religion. The Sikh Gurus condemned the Hindu caste system and they insisted on absolute equality for all, whether rich or poor, male or female.

The congregation (*sangat*) gathered early in the morning and again in the evening to sing the Guru's hymns and to listen to his discourses. The Sikhs were taught not to despise manual labour of any kind, and even today all classes of people will give of their labour freely to build temples, to cook and serve food in the *langar* and to clean the temple precincts.

Guru Angad was succeeded by eight more Gurus during the next 150 years. The fifth one, Guru Arjan, built the Golden Temple at Amritsar, which today is the holy city of the Sikhs. The Temple stands in the centre of a beautiful marble-lined pool, with a causeway leading across the lake to one of its four doors.

Most of the Gurus composed hymns and poetic works for use in prayer, meditation and ceremonies. Guru Arjan, who was a very fine and prolific poet himself, collected these works and compiled the *Guru Granth Sahib*, the Sikh holy book. In 1606, he died as a martyr, tortured at the command of the Emperor Jehangir,[1] because he refused

[1] The line of Mogul emperors which at that time ruled India was founded by Babar who invaded in 1526. Some of the emperors, like Jehangir and Aurangzeb, were fanatical Moslems who tried to impose Islam on all and sundry. Others, like Akbar (1542–1605), were tolerant of other faiths. The Mogul empire finally broke up about 1738.

to alter in the holy book a verse to which Jehangir objected.

The ninth Guru was also martyred, beheaded in 1675 by Emperor Aurangzeb, because he asserted the rights of the Hindus to follow their own religion.

The last Guru was Guru Gobind Singh who created the Khalsa Brotherhood in April 1699. *Khalsa* means 'pure' and the Sikhs were to become saint-soldiers. Five loyal Sikhs who had proved themselves willing to sacrifice their lives for the Guru became the founder members of the *Khalsa*. The Guru called them the Five Beloved Ones (*Panch Pyare*). He then baptised them by a ceremony which is still observed today. He prepared water in a steel bowl, reciting over it five prayers while stirring it with a double-edged sword. His wife added sweets to the water. Then he sprinkled it five times on the hair and eyes of the Five and gave them some of it to drink. He commanded them always to wear five symbols whose names begin with K: the uncut hair, *Keshas*; a comb, *Kangha*; a steel bangle, *Kara*; a pair of shorts, *Kachcha*; and a short sword, *Kirpan*. They were to adopt a common surname, Singh, meaning lion, to symbolise their brotherhood in one family and their repudiation of their former caste. They were forbidden to cut their hair, to smoke tobacco or to take intoxicants. They must not commit adultery nor should they eat meat of an animal which has been slaughtered by bleeding it slowly to death. The Sikhs were instructed to fight in righteous causes and to defend the weak against tyranny. They were to worship the One God and to love each other as brothers. Having baptised the Five, the Guru caused them to baptise him also, and in this way he demonstrated their equality with him. This baptism of *Amrit* (nectar) he offered to all the Sikhs, including women, who thereupon assumed the surname Kaur, meaning princess.

Women were to adopt the same symbols as the men and they were expected to conform to the same rules, having absolute equality in all religious and secular matters.

Guru Gobind Singh lost all four of his sons, the elder two in battle against hopeless odds, while the two younger boys were captured and killed by the governor of Sirhind. The Guru died in 1708, at Nanded in Hyderabad, having been stabbed by an assassin. Before he died, he ordained that there were to be no more living Gurus, but that the Granth Sahib should be regarded as the spiritual teacher, and the Khalsa should henceforth be the living representative of the Ten Gurus.

CUSTOMS AND PRACTICES

The martial training which Guru Gobind Singh gave to the Sikhs and the many struggles which they had to face during their subsequent history have helped to make them an adventurous and enterprising people. Perhaps this accounts for the fact that there are now numerous well-established Sikh communities in so many parts of the world outside the Punjab. Wherever they have settled, they have installed the Guru Granth Sahib in their homes and in temples.

The Sikh Temple is known as a *gurdwara*. It is generally organised by an elected committee. Although there is no class of trained or ordained priesthood in Sikhism, a *granthi* is usually appointed whose duty it is to conduct ceremonies when required, to read the Guru Granth Sahib, to welcome guests, and to take care of the building from day to day. Any Sikh man or woman may conduct ceremonies, sing hymns or speak in the gurdwara.

The Guru Granth Sahib is always ceremonially installed and treated with the utmost reverence. It is placed on cushions on a dais, covered in rich cloths, with a canopy above it, while the reader presides on a lower cushion, occasionally waving over it a ceremonial long-haired whisk, as was the ancient custom for monarchs. The members of the congregation enter its presence with covered heads and shoes removed. They bow low before the dais and respectfully place on the cloth an offering of money, which is used for religious purposes. The coverings are removed reverently whenever the volume is to be read, and when it has to be moved, it is carried on the bearer's head, still carefully wrapped.

Four principal ceremonies mark the life of a Sikh. The parents of a new baby take it to the gurdwara during the service and when the Guru Granth Sahib is opened at random for a reading at the end, they note the first letter which begins the verse on the left of the page. This letter must be the initial of the child's name which they choose in the presence of the congregation. Sikh names can belong to either a boy or a girl and they are distinguished only by the surname of Singh or Kaur. Thus, a girl may be Amrit Kaur and a boy may be Amrit Singh. Because of the confusion caused by having so many surnames of Singh, it has become the practice for some Sikhs to use another surname derived from their ancestral caste, or occupation or village.

Those Sikhs who wish to adhere strictly to the rules of the Khalsa must undergo the baptism ceremony which is the same as that instituted by Guru Gobind Singh. It must be performed by five baptised (*amritdhari*) Sikhs, and the initiates must be mature enough to understand the meaning and obligations of the religion and the necessity for keeping the five Ks afterwards. Ideally, young people should not be baptised until after the age of fourteen.

The institution of marriage was greatly respected by the Sikh Gurus, who valued family life as a natural and right way of life even for the most religious and unworldly people. In their hymns the Gurus often refer to the human soul as being the bride of the eternal Husband, God. Thus earthly marriage symbolises the union of the spirit of man with the divine Lord, and ideally the husband and wife in a Sikh marriage should try to reach a state of spiritual and mental harmony with each other. Guru Ram Das composed the four verses of the marriage hymn to celebrate his own marriage to Bibi Bhani, the daughter of the third Guru. It forms the central part of the Sikh marriage ceremony, in which the young couple encircle the Guru Granth Sahib four times, once to each of the verses of the marriage hymn (*Lavan*).

On the death of a Sikh, his body is cremated and at the funeral the relatives may read some appropriate hymns with a brief service. Afterwards there would generally be a religious service at home or in the gurdwara and there may be a continuous reading of the Guru Granth Sahib performed by relays of readers.

In Britain, and in other Western countries, the Sikhs congregate at the gurdwara every Sunday, usually in the morning but sometimes, as at the Central Gurdwara in London, in the late afternoon. The service begins with hymns led by individual singers to the accompaniment of the drums (*tabla*) and a small harmonium, while the congregation may join in. No chairs are allowed in the gurdwara so that everybody sits on the carpet, while according to the usual custom—though it is not a religious requirement—men and women sit separately. The hymns may be followed by a speaker who may tell a story, preach a sermon or make announcements, and the service is concluded with six verses of the Song of Joy (*Anand*) and the Sikh Prayer (*Ardas*). The *Anand* is chanted by the whole congregation, while everybody stands for the *Ardas* which is said by the granthi standing before the Guru Granth Sahib. To conclude, the holy volume is reverently opened and a verse is read from a page chosen at random; this verse is considered to be of special significance for that particular moment. When the service is over, everyone in the sangat is given the sacred sweet (*karah prashad*) which must be received in both hands cupped together. In the tradition of the Guru's free kitchen, food is also served, although not in all the gurdwaras in Britain.

On special anniversaries, celebrating Baisakhi (the Gurus' birthdays or martyrdom days) there is a much larger and longer gathering than usual and special singers and speakers are invited. Sikhs in Britain usually celebrate Baisakhi, on the 13th April (or on a Sunday after that date), the martyrdom of Guru Arjan in June, the birthday of Guru Nanak in November, and the birthday of Guru Gobind Singh in late December or early January. Other celebrations may be arranged by the local gurdwara committees.

SIKHS IN BRITAIN

There are over fifty Sikh organisations in Britain and at least forty of these have their own gurdwara or regular hired hall. The largest settlements of Sikhs are in Southall, Woolwich, Gravesend, Birmingham, Walsall, Wolverhampton, Nottingham, Coventry and Leeds, with others in similar industrial areas. Many of the people are factory workers, but there are also many white-collar workers and professional people such as teachers, scientists, nurses, doctors, accountants, architects, engineers, dentists and barristers, as well as others with their own private businesses.

Despite the fact that some Sikh children arrive in school with a poor command of English, they generally prove to be very good scholars because education and industry are highly valued. As the Sikhs in India are generally farmers or connected with the land, they have supported the protection of cattle, not because the cow is sacred to them as it is to the Hindus, but out of economic necessity. Because of this, few Sikhs will eat beef. In the Punjab, the meat most commonly eaten is goat and chicken, and Punjabi food includes much milk and milk products, pulses (*dhall*), unleavened bread made from unrefined wheat flour, as well as vegetables, spices and fruits.

The only items which Sikhs are obliged to wear for religious reasons are the 5 Ks, but Sikh men and boys, who keep the long hair, must wear the turban which is regarded as equally important with the symbols themselves. Young men may take off the turban for sports, securing the hair with a small cloth. The *kachcha* (shorts) are replaced by ordinary underwear these days, while the *kirpan* is usually worn only as a small symbol set into the wooden comb or as a brooch or badge.

As is the case with other communities, Sikhs as individuals naturally vary widely in the degree of commitment to the forms of their faith. One Sikh may rise at dawn to meditate, as his religious instructions recommend, and insist on every detail of the five Ks. Another, however, may be quite indifferent to his religion. Naturally there are more people who come somewhere in between the two extremes. Wherever they stand, however, they will inevitably show those qualities of character which have been cultivated by their original Sikh religion and culture, with its emphasis on religious reverence and its practical humanitarian approach to life

FOR FURTHER READING:

Harbans Singh: *Guru Nanak* (Asia Publishing House).
Khushwant Singh: *Sacred Writings of the Sikhs* (Allen and Unwin).
McLeod: *The Sikhs of the Punjab* (Oriel Press).
McLeod: *Guru Nanak and the Sikh Religion* (O.U.P.).
P. M. Wylam: *An Introduction to Sikh Belief* (pamphlet).
P. M. Wylam: *Brief Outline of the Sikh Faith* (pamphlet).

Mrs. P. M. Wylam, 17 Abbotshall Road, Catford, London S.E.6.

The Sikh Cultural Society of Great Britain, 88 Mollison Way, Edgware, Middlesex.

The Central Gurdwara, 62 Queensdale Road, Norland Castle, London W. 11.

Postscript

No attempt will be made here at a 'comparative study' of the various religions which are described. It is of course impossible not to notice some similarities as well as differences—for instance, in the conception of God as held by Hindus and by Jews, the ethical principles of Buddhism and of Christianity, the practices of Muslims and of Sikhs. But it would be quite out of place in a book of this kind to pick out features of one religious system in order to compare them with aspects of another. This is the highly specialised subject known as the 'comparative study of religions'. If this is undertaken in a superficial manner it is as inappropriate and impertinent as it would be to attempt to 'compare and contrast' Westminster Abbey and the Taj Mahal. Each has a splendour and a beauty of its own and to make a detailed 'comparative study' of the two would be to destroy our appreciation of both. So with the great world religions, it is surely preferable to view each as a whole and seek to enter into the spirit of those who profess it.

The various contributions to this book illustrate the difficulty of arriving at a definition of 'religion'. Perhaps the most fitting assessment is that given by one (Miss Marghanita Laski) who is avowedly of no religion, who has compared the enjoyment and appreciation of music with the religious experience, the essence of both being that they lift us above our usual selves. The contributors to this book would add '. . . and bring us into contact with ultimate reality'. If this book has enabled readers to appreciate how this is conceived by people of different traditions or races and has given some understanding of their approach to life and its problems, it will have achieved its purpose.

H.A.G.

A Table of Dates

The dates of the world's leading religious figures are given here, together with those of some other events of world-wide or national importance.

B.C.:

2000–1500	The founding of Hinduism.
c. 1700	Abraham, the father of the Hebrews.
c. 1500	The building of Stonehenge.
c. 1250	Moses, the founder of the Jewish Law.
c. 1180	The capture of Troy by the Greeks.
c. 1100	The Chou dynasty in China.
753 (traditional)	The founding of Rome.
c. 571–479	Confucius.
c. 560–480	Gotama the Buddha.
c. 500	Lao-Tzu, the founder of Taoism.
470–399	Socrates.
427–347	Plato.

A.D.:

30/33	The crucifixion of Jesus of Nazareth.
70 and 135	The destruction of Jerusalem by the Romans.
570–632	Mohammad.
1469–1539	Nanak, the founder of Sikhism.

Index

Ahimsa, 19f
Amritsar, 123
Animism, 40, 53, 62f
Arabia, 107
Ashoka, 19, 36
Avtaras, 12

Bhagavad Gita, 5f
Brahma, 9, 10, 18

Caste, 17, 25, 125
Chanukkah, 29
Confucian Humanism, 50f
Confucius, 40ff
Constantine, 97

Emperor, Chinese, 55f
Emperor, Japanese, 64f

God, 10ff, 35, 40, 53, 55, 71, 75,
   91, 99, 105, 108, 111, 122ff
Gotama, 23ff, 35
Granth, 125, 127f
Gurus, 124f

Hebrews, 70ff
Hijrah, 109f

Ise, 63f
Islam, 104

Japan, 62ff
Jesus, 84, 90ff

Karma, 7f, 32f
Krishna, 6, 13

Lao-Tzu, 44

Mahabharata, 5
Mecca, 109, 114
Messiah, 89, 94
Mishnah, 74
Mohammad, 108ff

Nanak, 122ff
Neo-Confucianism, 49f
Nirvana, 27, 32f
Noble Eightfold Path, 29ff
Noble Truths, 27ff

Passover, 78, 95
Pentecost, 78f, 96

Quran, 106

Ramadhan, 113
Ramayana, 4f

Singh, 126

Talmud, 74
Taoism, 44, 47, 53
Transmigration, 8ff
Trinity, 98

Upanishads, 3f, 25

Vedas, 2f, 25
Vishnu, 5, 10